The Mentalization Guidebook

The Mentalization Guidebook

Janne Østergaard Hagelquist

KARNAC

First printed in Danish in 2015 by Hans Reitzels Forlag

First printed in English in 2017 by
Karnac Books Ltd
118 Finchley Road
London NW3 5HT

Translated from the Danish by Ray Weaver

British Library Cataloguing in Publication Data

A C.I.P. for this book is available from the British Library

ISBN-13: 978-1-78220-417-6

Typeset by V Publishing Solutions Pvt Ltd., Chennai, India

Printed in Great Britain by TJ International Ltd, Padstow, Cornwall

www.karnacbooks.com

Contents

Preface *by Peter Fonagy* 9
Organisation of the Guidebook 11
Flowchart. 12
Introduction 17
   Mentalization 18
     The dimensions of mentalization 22
     Mentalization failure and pre-mentalization modes 24
     Mentalization difficulties and assessment of the ability
       to mentalize 26
   Mentalization and treatment. 26
     An Open (ÅBENT) mind 28
     The STORM model 30
     The intervention spectrum. 38
     Natural developmental interactions 41
     The integrated model – the building blocks of mentalization
       in teaching and therapy. 43

Part 1: Theory and analysis

Mentalization

Mentalization 49
Balancing between the dimensions of mentalization 51
Mentalizing failure. 54
Mentalizing failure – early forms of mentalization. 56
Mentalization difficulties 58

Analysis – treatment

Assessment of mentalizing ability in adults – a scale of
   reflexive function. 60
Mentalization and learning 64
Attachment patterns. 66
An Open (ÅBENT) mind. 68

The STORM model. 71
Obtaining skills. 75
The intervention spectrum 78
Mentalization in family therapy – MBT-F loop 80
Contingent mirroring and deviant mirroring styles. 82
The integrative model – the building blocks of mentalization
    in teaching and in therapy. 86

Neglect – symptoms
Neglect. 88
Symptoms of violence – active physical neglect. 90
Symptoms of sexual abuse – active physical neglect 92
Symptoms of psychological abuse – active mental
    neglect. 94
Symptoms of neglect – passive physical neglect 96
Symptoms of a lack of development enhancing interactions – passive
    mental neglect. 98

Part 2: Psycho-education
Mentalization
Mentalization and psycho-education 103
The emotional compass as psycho-education 106

Trauma
Diagnostic criteria for PTSD 109
PTSD in children 115
Developmental trauma. 117
How you as a parent can help your traumatised child. 119
MacLean's triune brain theory 122
Fight, flight, freeze. 125
Protective factors in trauma 128

Dynamics
Lies. 130
The dynamics of transgenerational trauma. 132
Chaos and rigidity 134
The victim–persecutor–rescuer triangle 136

Part 3: Tools for the professional

Self-reflection at the time

The OPEN thermometer 141
The three questions 143
The breathing space 145

Self-reflection afterwards

Mentalizing failure and self-reflection. 147
Pseudo-mentalization 151
Paths to maintaining reflection and calm with balance
      and support 153

Part 4: Exercises

Security

Security – creating security 159
Security – treating stress 161
Security – angels in the nursery 163
Security – sleep. 165
Security – exercise for falling asleep 167

Trauma focus

Trauma focus – the survivor knight. 171
Trauma focus – trigger analysis 174
Trauma focus – the 90/10 response. 176
Trauma focus – the brain's alarm system. 178
Trauma focus – re-enactment. 181
Trauma focus – ghosts in the nursery. 185
Trauma focus – overcoming trauma 187

Obtaining skills

Obtaining skills – emotions – what is inside your body 189
Obtaining skills – emotions – the compass of emotions 191
Obtaining skills – emotions – talking about emotions/a game
      with basic emotions 193
Obtaining skills – emotions – crisis plan 196
Obtaining skills – emotions – sadness volume control button 200

Obtaining skills – emotions – joy volume control button 202
Obtaining skills – emotions – anger volume control button 204
Obtaining skills – emotions – fear volume control button 206
Obtaining skills – emotions – symptoms of anxiety 208
Obtaining skills – emotions – anxiety hierarchy 210
Obtaining skills – behaviour – strategies for regulating behaviour 213
Obtaining skills – behaviour – pros and cons 215
Obtaining skills – behaviour – chain analysis 217
Obtaining skills – behaviour – reflect and repair 220
Obtaining skills – behaviour – mentalized boundary setting 222
Obtaining skills – attention/cognition 224
Obtaining skills – physical – registering body sensations 226
Obtaining skills – self – what is happening inside your head? 228
Obtaining skills – self – the inside and outside of a box 231
Obtaining skills – self – brain scan 234
Obtaining skills – self – life stories 236
Obtaining skills – relationships – brain scan for parents and child 238
Obtaining skills – relations – family tree 241
Obtaining skills – relationships – the network circle 243
Obtaining skills – relationships – a yin and yang balance 245

Resource focus
Resource focus – the shield of self-esteem 247
Resource focus – dreams for the future 249

Mentalization
Mentalization – doctor: what happens in the minds of others? 251
Mentalization – the hunt for mental states 252
Mentalization – role play 253
Mentalization – the journalist game 254
Mentalization – spin the bottle 255
Mentalization – my boundaries 256
Mentalization – thought bubbles 258
Mentalization – the dream journey 260

References 263
About the author 267

Preface

Peter Fonagy

The theory and practice of mentalizing address the bedrock human capacity to understand mind as such. Given how fundamental it is to human relatedness and self-awareness, you might think that we require no training, no "easy access" guide to achieve what is built into our nature. And yet there is so much in our culture which compromises this most basic of human capacities that a book of this kind is not just desirable; it is essential.

It is a platitude to say that we have less time for each other, and particularly for our children, than we used to. It is a fact, however, that we spend less time eating together as families, teaching our children the basic skills that would help them thrive in human society, that we interact through very restricted channels of communication – by text message, by social media, and shared experience of television programmes – rather than joint adventures and common activities. No one would argue that children can learn to truly understand affect through emoticons. The subtlety and complexity of human life is so readily reduced to a two-dimensional image by the constraints that twenty-first-century living places on all of us.

I guess it has always been thus, but perhaps in past epochs it was hunger, disease, and wars that undermined our ability to think about each other as intentional agents, to contemplate the multilayered understanding of others' intentions and feelings. And now that we have made massive progress in relation to these historical enemies of civilisation, we have created fresh limitations that are just as powerful and just as limiting. Education is now universal, but we teach children and adolescents in large classes and restrict the amount of social time they spend in the company of adults. Other children become their primary socialising agents. We are appropriately disdainful and disapproving of the nineteenth-century attitudes towards child labour. Yet apprenticeships, however exploitative, enabled the young generation to spend time with the old, and in that contact they had an opportunity to observe how those with skills and competences performed. And, more importantly, to feel that as trainees they were an integral part of the continuity of a *community* as well as a trade. In the modern world, in the absence of adult guides, children and young people have to invent themselves and create their own culture, from which we as grown-ups are excluded.

This is not a complaint about modern times and an idealisation of days long gone. It is simply trying to explain why, notwithstanding the relative wealth of our society, a book which provides a very practical guide to treating children who have suffered adversity and are particularly disadvantaged is vital. I and colleagues have found, working in this field for the past quarter-century, that children who suffer maltreatment, whose needs, thoughts, and feelings are neglected, whose concerns are systematically ignored, have difficulty in treating others with the human dignity that they in turn deserve. This should not surprise anyone. The social context in which we live will activate particular patterns of behaviour that are most adaptive in that type of situation. If I am not thought about, if people have no time for me, maybe this is a context in which I do not need to prioritise finding time for other people. If my caregivers harbour actively hostile thoughts about me, maybe I am best off not thinking about what people think at all. I am sure we all find that attitude rational, even if not reasonable. And probably there is no "evil" in either the neglecting caregiver or the destructive, violent young person; both have adapted to a social situation where thinking about feelings, fostering the capacity to mentalize, is felt as irrelevant, risky, and perhaps even dangerous.

So what is this book about? It is a piece of psycho-education that "teaches" something that we should not need to learn. Who should read this book? Basically, all of us who from time to time have difficulty remembering why people do things. Parents who find themselves being irritated with their children; therapists who feel frustrated with their patients; managers who have difficulty in being compassionate with their staff, and staff who feel persecuted by management; teachers who have unruly classrooms; and all those who are confronted by emotional reactions in others which they have difficulty comprehending.

Thirty years ago, the concept of mentalizing emerged simultaneously out of cognitive science and psychoanalytic psychotherapy. Since then, many books have been written about the development of mentalizing and its application in different clinical and social contexts. What makes this book unique is that it tries to mentalize the reader somewhat more than other books on this topic. It communicates the subject in a way that is easy to follow and accessible to non-professionals and professionals alike. The illustrations help reduce the abstract content and perhaps excessive intellectualisation that can characterise books on this subject to something that through the medium of visual presentation becomes immediately obvious and concrete for the reader.

The author is to be congratulated for working hard to translate some quite esoteric concepts into something that is immediate and obvious to the human mind, much like "holding mind in mind" and relatedness and self-awareness are.

Peter Fonagy, PhD, FBA, FMedSci, OBE
Professor and head, Research Department of Clinical, Educational and Health Psychology, University College London; chief executive, Anna Freud Centre, London, UK

Organisation of the Guidebook

The purpose of this book is to provide inspiration for using mentalization when working with vulnerable children, adolescents, and their families. It is also designed to assist professionals with applying and maintaining mentalization-based teaching and therapy when working with those at risk.

The book provides, among other things, specific educational tools and models that relate to the essential concepts discussed in the book's introduction. These specific tools can be helpful in a professional's daily work. At the same time, it is important to keep in mind that the professional's own mentalizing abilities are the primary educational or therapeutic tool.

Mentalization-based treatment is about ensuring long-term development in children. This is done by building a relationship with the child and becoming more adept at looking deeper into and understanding the child's behaviour and thus helping the child or the family to understand themselves better.

Mentalization-based treatment does not focus directly on enhancing insights and treatment is not specifically aimed at changing behaviours. The activity of reflection is the object (Skårderud & Sommerfeldt, 2014). The mentalization-based way of thinking is traditionally very sceptical of therapists who think they know how a child or adolescent is feeling or how they think. Instead, the focus is on creating a safe environment and stimulating the mentalization process.

It is important that this guidebook does not become something that comes between the caregiver and the child or young person. The guide is meant to be used as a tool. It is to be shared, and the purpose is always to help both oneself and the other person to understand themselves and the other better. The book is not intended as an inflexible set of rules, where the models become rigid categories that limit curiosity and forget that the mind is complex. The desire is that this book should complement playful, exceptional, and explorative interactions. Use these models for inspiration and/or create your own – but never let the models become more important than the understanding of the child.

The remainder of the book is made up of four parts, each with models and tools for working with vulnerable children, adolescents, and their families.

Part 1: Theory and analysis includes the basic models of mentalization, which creates an overview of the theory and can specifically be used in the analysis of a child, adolescent, or family.

Part 2: Psycho-education provides ways to support the neglected and traumatised to find a better understanding of themselves and their struggles. The models within can be used in teaching or directly in therapy.

Flowchart

This flowchart can help you to choose the section that applies to your needs.

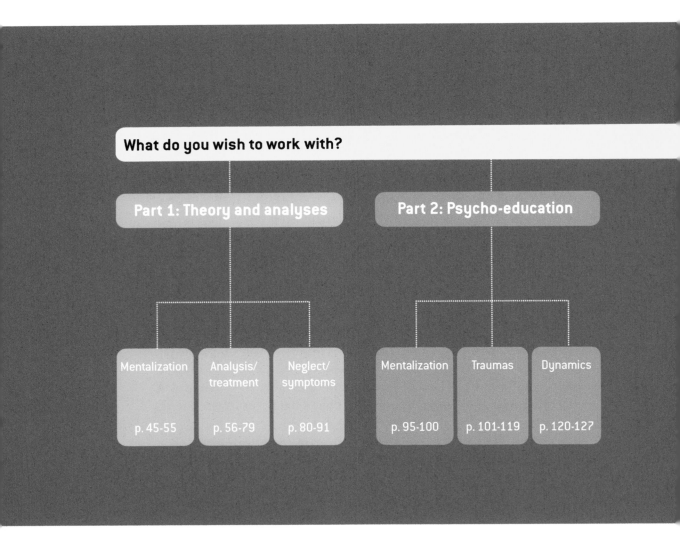

Part 3: Tools for the professional helps practitioners reflect on themselves. In mentalization, the professionals' ability to create peace in their own mind and to understand their own mental condition is central to creating the most effective treatment.

Part 4: Exercises contains practical and useful tools for treatment. This part is based on the STORM model, so there are treatment tools for each of the five processing elements: Security, Trauma focus, Obtaining skills, Resources, and Mentalization.

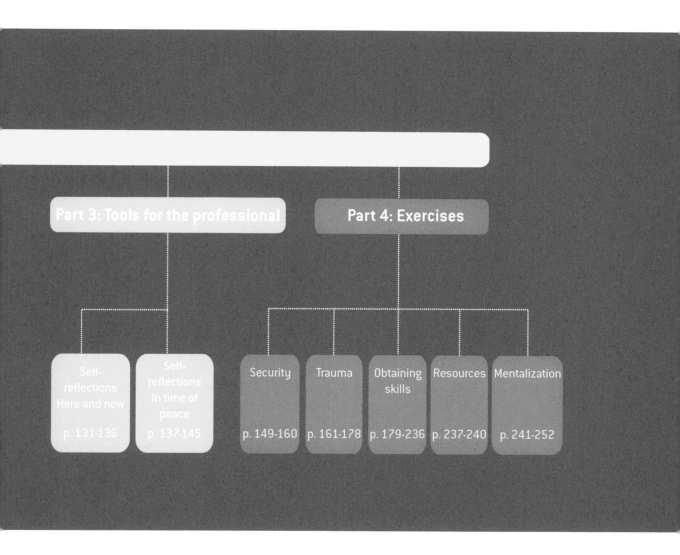

The introduction sheet for each model provides a quick overview of the model's origin and applications. Each sheet has three support headings, and offers the best tips and tricks for each model. There is an anonymous practice example with each sheet:

	What do you do? Includes ideas on how the model can be applied in practice. Since this is not intended as an inflexible manual, there are no inflexible templates or rules, just ideas on how to use each model.
	Tips and tricks These are tips and tricks obtained by myself and my colleagues, through practical experience on how to use the specific model or avoid potential pitfalls.
	Examples All models are illustrated with a small case history that elaborates and puts into perspective the model's uses and effects.

The key points of the models are:

- All models are for use in mentalization conversations. It is not a manual, but rather a framework of ideas on how using humour, flexibility, and games may make one better at mentalizing. In Vygotsky's words: "In play a child always behaves beyond his average age, above his daily behavior; in play it is as though he were a head taller than himself" (Fonagy, Gergely, Jurist, & Target, 2007, p. 248).

- The caregiver must find her (or his, of course, but single pronouns will be used throughout, referring to either gender) own personal and authentic way in which to use the guide. In the following example, a child shows an adult exactly how the guide should *not* be used. An educator who had attended a mentalization course came home and started using the guide and language of the course. The child was upset by this new approach and said to the teacher: "Now, please be yourself again."

- Mentalization is about being aware of one's own mental state and that of others. The practitioner must also be able to master the delicate balance of maintaining objectivity and examining while not forgetting her knowledge of mentalization, development, and trauma. Both education and therapy are viewed as educational relationships, that is, there is someone who knows more than the other person – so that one person can teach the other. Here is an example of using the guide. A young woman says to her foster mother, "Mentalization is all well and good, but my need to smoke hash before I come home tonight is just as important as your needs." To which the foster mother replies, "It is true that we both have needs, and I understand yours, but as an adult, I have a better grasp on what is best in the long run. I want you to be home before 11pm and I do not want you to smoke hash."

Introduction

Over the past several years, I have learned that it can be of benefit to use the mentalization approach both in the therapeutic and educational treatment of neglected and traumatized children and adolescents and their families. I have found that the value of paying attention to the mental states lying behind neglected and traumatised children's behaviour cannot be stressed enough. Furthermore, it is my experience that maintaining an awareness of your own (and your colleagues') mental states as a professional working with children and adolescents at risk is equally important.

When I teach mentalization and trauma, I often note that professionals perceive that the concept makes sense because it reflects what they do in their everyday lives. At the same time, they have said that a model and specific ideas concerning application makes it even easier to relate the theory to the challenges that they face in everyday life. Through supervision of cases involving children and adolescents, I have learned that the theoretical concepts of mentalization-based treatment are effective in raising the awareness of children and adolescents, and they are useful in analysing which treatment is beneficial for a particular child or family. I have also seen that there is a great desire for readily available models to help vulnerable children and adolescents to better understand themselves. I have often shared the models I use when supervising. Many have expressed the desire for a comprehensive and clear overview of the models and practical tools that I use to work with vulnerable children, adolescents, and their families.

These requests are what led me to write this book, which is a guide to mentalization. It is intended as a tool for professionals working with children and adolescents who want to use mentalization in their work. My hope is this book will present a digestible overview of the best concepts of mentalization and trauma psychology. I want to share those models and tools, along with the best tips and tricks that we in the Center for Mentalization use in our daily practice. This guide is based on my two previous books: *Mentalization in Encounters with Vulnerable Children* and *Mentalization in Pedagogy and Therapy*. These books could be a useful read before starting to use this guide.

This book is structured so that the introductory chapter provides a refresher on mentalization theory and the well-known concepts described in my previous books. In the same chapter, I also review the central processing models used in mentalization-based teaching and therapy. Research in mentalization and trauma is developing rapidly, which means that there is constantly new knowledge about how to understand oneself and help others understand themselves. In the first chapter, I will go beyond a simple brush up on existing knowledge and pay particular attention to some of the new things happening in the field.

Mentalization

The central concept of this book is mentalization, a concept that was originally developed in psychotherapy. The Hungarian-born psychologist Peter Fonagy and his colleagues have given it new life in recent decades, so that today it is also useful in everyday encounters with vulnerable children, adolescents, and their families. Mentalization can be defined in different ways. One definition is "a focus on mental states in oneself and in others, especially in connection with the explanation of behavior" (Bateman & Fonagy, 2007, p. 33). The mental conditions that affect behaviour, emotions, needs, goals, reasons, and thoughts. The very short-term and more idiomatic way to define mentalization is to "keep the mind in mind" (Allen, Fonagy, & Bateman, 2010, p. 26). Using mentalization and the associated theories can, as it has always done, result in excellent treatment, but it has often lacked a language and thus the academic credentials to be fully conceptualised.

In the following example, mentalization is used by a foster mother and foster father:

Caroline, who is fourteen years old, has lived with her foster parents since she was three months old. Her biological parents are addicts. Caroline had contact with her father during her adolescence, and has always idealised her father. Even though he is an active addict and has failed Caroline repeatedly and embarrassed her often, she always makes excuses for him and is very sensitive to her foster parents' cautious remarks that he has sometimes made things difficult.

When Caroline is scheduled to go to a handball summer camp to Sweden, she agrees with her biological father to meet and say goodbye the night before she leaves. When he does not turn up, she expresses for the first time how disappointed she is in her father. Her foster mother listens and is very happy that Caroline finally has the courage to talk about the disappointments that her father has caused her. She is proud that Caroline has finally found the confidence to put words to her disappointment.

Caroline's foster mother and father do everything they can to make the day she leaves for camp a good one. On the day she is scheduled to leave, they wake up early and make her lunch and arrange the final details. Caroline's biological father shows up at the last minute. He is half-stoned, but has brought along an adolescent magazine for Caroline to read on the trip. Caroline hugs him and repeats over and over again, "You are the best dad in the world, I wish I could stay with you." This all takes place just before they have to leave and catch the bus. When Caroline's foster father gently suggests that it is time to leave, Caroline responds by shouting at him to "shut his fucking mouth and not ruin everything".

Caroline's foster mother is frustrated and feels very angry inside. She remembers what she has read about mentalization and realises that Caroline cannot bear to have both an argument and an unhappy separation from her father directly before a trip abroad without adults. The foster mother can also see that Caroline needs to feel that she has a positive relationship with her foster parents before she leaves. This means that the foster mother will have to tone down her anger to deal with the situation, so that Caroline can say a positive goodbye to her father. In the car on the way to the bus, Caroline's foster mother says, "If I was travelling and struck a situation between people that I care about, I would do everything I could to make sure not to escalate the conflict and try to make everyone feel good. I do not know whether that was why you reacted the way you did, but it makes perfect sense to me." The foster mother continues, "But that still does not make it ok to say 'shut your fucking mouth'. It hurts me when you talk like that, but I still want you to know that I love you and I will miss you." The incident ends with Caroline climbing happily on the bus.

In this case, Caroline's foster mother is aware that Caroline's mental state is the reason for her behaviour. She understands that Caroline needs to feel close to her father before she travels so far from home. The foster mother realises that when she says "shut your fucking mouth" to her foster father, is it because there are many intense feelings going on inside her that she cannot control. The foster mother is also aware that Caroline's behaviour unleashes feelings and thoughts inside her. She chooses not to act on them in the moment, but wait for the intensity of the situation to diminish for both Caroline and herself.

There are three key reasons in this case why it is important to mentalize and why treatment focusing on mentalization techniques is appropriate (Allen, Bleiberg, & Haslam-Hopwood, 2003):

1. Through mentalizing one's own feelings, one can learn to know one's own thoughts and assumptions and understand that they are the reason for one's behaviour. It creates a sense of being in control of one's actions and creates self-awareness and a sense of identity.

2. Mentalizing is the basis for meaningful, sustaining relationships. By mentalizing, one sees the other person's perspective, while also making it possible to hold on to who one is inside a relationship. This is the cornerstone of healthy relationships.

3. Mentalizing is the key to regulating one's self and emotions.

In this case, Caroline's foster mother looks beyond her own emotions to see that Caroline has finally started to verbalise her frustration at her father's repeated failures. The foster mother realises that seeing her father fail so often over the years has been hard on Caroline. This self-knowledge gives her a sense of being in control of her own actions, and provides self-awareness and a sense of identity. The foster mother at once sees her own, her husband's, Caroline's, and the biological father's perspective, making it possible for her to maintain a positive relationship with all the parties involved.

The foster mother realises that Caroline's behaviour is an expression of her desire to protect herself and to try to create harmony before she leaves. This makes it possible for the foster mother to wind down her own anger.

The foster mother also shows, during the conversation in the car, that she is well aware that the mind is opaque and that we humans never completely know the basis for the actions of others when she says, "I do not know whether that was why you reacted the way you did". This is at the heart of mentalization; that it is non-mentalizing to be too sure of what you or other people think and feel (Ryden & Wallroth, 2010, p. 238).

In this case, it was clear that mentalization may be central to working with vulnerable people. But the concept is actually key not only when it comes to neglected and traumatised people with a diagnosis, but also for people with no traumatic history – thus, it is about both them and us. The theory of mentalization is about being human and managing one's self, relationships, and emotions, making it a valuable guidance mechanism for anyone.

Mentalization theory makes it possible to discuss how people who have experienced neglect and trauma have missed the positive development interactions that could have assisted them in developing their own mentalizing abilities, and how trauma can lead to fragile mentalizing abilities that can easily collapse. The theory is based on normal development and describes how everyone experiences mentalizing failures and how mentalization can be further developed in everyone throughout their lives.

When a child has been exposed to neglect and trauma, he will not have the basics needed to develop mentalizing abilities. It is believed that the ability to mentalize can be developed through interaction with more mature and sensitive minds (Midgley & Vrouva, 2012). Mentalizing begets mentalizing. Therefore, the fundamental tool in working with vulnerable adolescents is to "keep the mind in mind". It is crucial to support the child and ensure that treatment includes understanding the feelings, thoughts, and intentions beneath the child/adolescent's actions. Sometimes it can be difficult to understand the mental conditioning underlying a neglected child's behaviour, and it can be difficult for children who have suffered neglect and trauma to verbalise their feelings and thoughts.

The dimensions of mentalization

Mentalization is a multifaceted ability with several dimensions. Some people may have deficiencies in some of these dimensions, but not in others. There can also be imbalances within and between dimensions. It is important to pay attention to the combination of individual mentalization abilities during analysis and treatment.

Mentalization can be divided onto four dimensions, and various forms of mental illness can be understood as an imbalance in these dimensions (Bateman & Fonagy, 2012):

1. Automatic/implicit or controlled/explicit
2. Self/other
3. Cognitive/affective
4. Inner-focused/outer-focused

We balance the first dimension naturally in everyday life. In our daily interaction, automatic mentalization is dominant, but when we do not understand each other, the controlled version takes over. Automatic mentalization is what we do when we are together and naturally seem to understand each other. This form of mentalization is reflexive, instinctive, and unintentional. When we suddenly feel that another's behaviour no longer makes sense, and we try to discern the reason for his actions, we switch to controlled mentalization. Controlled mentalization is a relatively slow process, requiring language, reflection, and an active mental effort. In the following example, it is clear how necessary this balance is – especially when working with neglected and traumatised children and adolescents.

A teacher at a special school for disadvantaged children is teaching biology. He is teaching the mating habits of frogs. The students are listening, interested. Then a boy says: "Then the male frog puts semen – a lot of semen, all over the eggs – that's how they are fertilized." Suddenly, a girl gets up and screams: "FUCK ALL OF YOU" and runs from the room.

The teacher uses his controlled mentalizing when he thinks, "Why is she acting like that?" He recalls that the girl has been sexually abused, and that the mention of semen may have been what triggered the reaction. He makes an agreement with the school head to meet with the girl. When the girl arrives for her next biology class, the teacher greets her as always – not as a girl who was the victim of a sexual assault – but as a child interested in salamanders, just like the rest of the class.

In the first part of the example, the teacher uses automatic mentalization. He is interested in teaching, and there is an agreed understanding that the class is about frogs. The mentalization is here quick and unconscious. When the girl gets up and leaves, automatic mentalization is suspended. The girl's behaviour no longer makes sense, and the teacher starts using his controlled mentalization abilities. When the girl returns for the next biology class, the teacher shows his flexibility at balancing between the two dimensions by reverting to automatic mentalization. Getting stuck in controlled mentalization is a trap. Most of us know how uncomfortable it is to be seen through the prism of controlled mentalization. If, for example, you are short-tempered with your partner and explain it by saying, "Forgive me, I was stressed out." from then on, in every situation, your partner says, "Of course, I understand. You are stressed out."

The balance is difficult for both lay people and professionals to maintain. Estimates are that a teacher makes five decisions per minute (Jacobsen, 2014). I dare not guess how many decisions are made in one minute, or how many shifts there are between automatic and controlled mentalizing, when a teacher or educator is working with vulnerable children and adolescents.

At the same time, the brain must also balance the other dimensions.

The second dimension deals with a balanced ability to reflect on and understand the intentions of both oneself and others. An imbalance occurs when one focuses only on the minds of others or, conversely, is only aware of one's own needs and intentions. Many professionals who work with vulnerable children and adolescents are at risk of being out of balance in these cases. It could be a foster mother who cares for a little boy. The boy has a history of trauma and diabetes. Consequently, during the first weeks with the new family, the child suffers repeatedly from insulin shock. The foster mother completely forgets her own needs. She mentalizes with the boy 24/7. She does not get enough sleep because she is up constantly checking the boy's blood sugar. If the foster mother does not get help so she can achieve balance and make room for her own needs, there is a risk that she will burn out and not be the kind of foster mother she wants to be for the rest of the boy's childhood.

The next dimension which must be balanced is the cognitive/affective dimension. Proper mentalization in this dimension is said to be the balance between reason and emotion. Ideally, mentalization integrates assumptions, thoughts, goals, and other cognitive mental states with feelings, desires, needs, and other affective mental states. This means that when a twenty-year-old woman considers marrying the mass murderer Anders Behring Breivik, she should strike a balance between her feelings, wants, and needs – as in, I think I may love him and want to believe that he has changed and he has plenty of time to write me love letters while sitting in prison. On the other hand, she also has more realistic ideas and assumptions about his ability to be a good husband.

The final inner-/outer-focused dimension is balanced when one is able to balance the mental states of oneself and others along with physical and visual modes. Bateman and Fonagy (2012) mention the narcissist as an example of an imbalance between the internal and external. The example included concerns a man with narcissistic traits who misses the signals being sent out by someone he is talking to. The partner yawns and desperately attempts to find someone else to talk to and continuously signals, "I cannot bear to hear any more." At the same time, the narcissist is overly concerned with the internal mentalizing of others; how they perceive him, if they are envious or admiring of him, and if they are aware of everything that he can do.

On page 52 is a model of the mentalization dimensions

Mentalization failure and pre-mentalization modes

Mentalization is a dynamic ability that is susceptible to stress and strong emotions. Therefore, it is difficult to maintain the practice of mentalization within close relationships. Mentalization failure occurs when one is no longer able to mentalize. Mentalization failure also occurs when intense emotions lead to brain-related changes that switch off mentalization skills (Bateman & Fonagy, 2012). Mentalization failure leads to the loss of focus on the mental states of oneself and others. One loses touch with both one's own feelings, needs, goals, and reasons and those of the other person. The ability to mentalize can be caused to fail by, for example, intense emotional arousal or perceived threat (Bateman & Fonagy, 2007).

Everyone can find themselves in situations where they do not have a perspective on what is happening inside either their own or other people's minds. Trauma and neglect result in reduced and fragile mentalization skills. Mentalization failure typically occurs in situations where the subject is experiencing high emotional intensity. This often occurs with people we are attached to and care about. In broad terms, we are weakest at mentalizing with those we love the most. Strong feelings and powerful emotions are mentalization's worst enemy.

During treatment, it is important to identify where mentalization is failing. In the model on page 55, mentalization failure is shown as a vessel where attention must be paid to the edge, where mentalization fails (just before the basin's edge goes straight down), and what happens when that failure continues (the bottom of the vessel) and when mentalization is on the way back up (the other side of the vessel) (Siegel & Hartzell, 2006).

During mentalization failure, one reverts to methods of mentalizing that developed before real mentalization. These techniques are called pre-mentalization methods. There are three types of early mentalization: the *teleological mode*, the *pretend mode*, and *psychic equivalency mode*.

The first mentalization skill developed is the *teleological mode*, which can be seen in infants as young as nine months old. They are able to attribute goals to other people and perceive things that seem to occur on the basis of will. The goal is not viewed as mental, but is more closely tied to the observable

(Allen & Fonagy, 2006, p. 85). Language does not really enter in here; we only accept physical actions as evidence of others' intentions and only believe that it is possible to change other people's attitude through physical actions.

> If you do not come and get me now, it's because you do not love me, and every-thing we have had together means nothing.

The two other early mentalization techniques are *the pretend mode* and *psychic equivalency mode*. They develop almost simultaneously. In *pretend mode*, the mental state seems to be separated from reality, and it sounds as if one is using mentalization, but it lacks emotional resonance. The Fonagy group calls this kind of mentalization, where one is toying with reality, "bullshitting" (Bateman & Fonagy 2012, p. 515).

An example of *pretend mode* can be a girl who at the final conversation with her psychologist relates how she has come far during her therapy. She describes in psychological terms that she understands how she became the person she was, and how she overcame her history of abuse and has moved on and can now use the benefit of her experience to help other victims of trauma. As she relates all of this, her psychologist feels that it is like listening to a needle stuck in a groove. Although the psychologist would gladly accept the credit for the girl's fine words, she is more concerned about how she really feels.

This type of pre-mentalization mode is disconnected from reality and is the direct opposite of the final pre-mentalization mode, the *psychic equivalency mode*, where mental states are almost too real. This mode is also called "the inner and outer are the same" mode (Allen & Fonagy, 2006). This is very descriptive of this type of early mentalization, wherein the inner and the outer world are seen as the same. In this mental state, a person thinks that just because he or someone else is thinking something, it must be true.

This can be seen in the example of a wife who says to her husband, "Why didn't you get the garden sorted over the weekend. You don't care about me. All you've done the entire weekend is watch football." The man replies: "Why didn't you say you wanted me to work in the garden?" To which she responds, "You know that is what I wanted. Are you trying to provoke me?"

On page 57 is a summary of pre-mentalizing methods

Psychic equivalency occurs when the woman is convinced that her husband knows what she is thinking and feeling.

Mentalization difficulties and assessment of the ability to mentalize

Along with mentalization failure there are also difficulties in mentalizing. Difficulties in mentalizing are rooted in mentalization failure. But here we are especially concerned about appearances. This can be seen when it looks like the person is mentalizing, but where the mentalization is inappropriate. The two forms of difficulties in mentalizing presented here are the abuse of mentalization and pseudo-mentalization.

The abuse of mentalization happens when a person's mental state is used against him. This is often seen in the distortion of the feelings of others in order to protect one's own interests, and through cognitive empathic understanding, which also aims to safeguard one's own interests. It could be the psychopath who says to his wife, "You've said yourself that you are always destroying your relationships and that you bring out the worst in others. Look what you've done to me. You have ruined me and turned me into a violent man."

On page 59, you can read about inappropriate mentalization and pseudo-mentalization in practice.

Pseudo-mentalization is often seen during work with children and adolescents, where someone becomes locked into a method of understanding a child or adolescent. For example: "She is uncooperative," "She just wants attention," and "He's just trying to take advantage of me."

The assessment of mentalization abilities is a rapidly developing field. There are currently a variety of review methods for children, adolescents, and adults. The traditional way to examine unravelling mentalization abilities is through reflexive function (RF). Reflective function is a way to make specific mentalization abilities concrete and measurable. It is beyond the scope of this book to do a thorough review of the investigation of mentalization abilities or reflexive function, but on pages 62–63 there is a copy of Anne Blom Corlin's attempt to create a scale for the assessment of mentalization abilities in adults. This model can also be used as a type of "map" to navigate one's educational approach or therapy (derived from Karterud & Bateman, 2011).

Mentalization and treatment

Mentalization-based therapy and teaching is viewed as a learning relationship because people primarily learn about the world through social interaction – in contrast to animals, which primarily learn about the world through their five senses. A main aspect of mentalization-based teaching is to teach the child about his own mental state, while the child simultaneously learns about his caregiver's internal state.

In recent years, research in mentalization has been particularly concerned about what it takes to get one person to want to learn from another. Attention has particularly focused on the concept of *epistemic trust* (1st International Conference on Mentalization, London, 2013; Fonagy & Allison, 2014).

epistemic trust is about having the confidence that others sincerely wish you well and that they will teach you something you can use and that is valuable to you (Fonagy & Allison, 2014). The idea is that a child in a healthy relationship learns the trust and flexibility he needs to learn from others. The entire basis for building the confidence to learn from others is about the child feeling understood, that is, he is being mentalized. Due to neglect some children do not feel understood, because others have failed in terms of mentalization towards them. This is critical because it affects the child's confidence in future educators – be they school teachers, social workers, or foster parents. Some children are simply not able to enter into a learning relationship. They are not willing to accept new information from another person as being trustworthy, useful, or even relevant to them (Fonagy & Allison, 2014). This is because they have never felt understood by others and therefore do not believe that others can teach them anything.

> As a fifty-year-old male client once told me: "Nobody has ever touched me more than skin deep. I do not need psychologists and therapists. or anyone at all, really. The only person I trust is myself…"

These types of clients need to be taught that other people want to help them. There are three different approaches to learning. The first type is where the clients are immediately ready to learn. These clients may settle for internet therapy where there is no close relationship and the therapy is mostly learning-based. These clients are ready to listen to the teacher. For others, *epistemic trust* can be more complicated. Sometimes, they are ready to learn from others, while in other instances, a relationship must be restored before any learning is possible.

The model on page 65 (mentalization and learning) describes the different approaches to learning.

The last and most difficult clients are those that do not have a natural sense of *epistemic trust*. Work with clients of this type begins by giving them a feeling that their therapist understands them. This shows them that they can connect and listen to other people. For these clients, there is a long way to go before mentalization can begin. A teacher once very aptly said that it is as if the person needed "princess-like handling". In those who have not developed *epistemic trust*, one should be constantly aware of looking behind behaviours to understand the clients' feelings, thoughts, needs, goals, and reasons.

It may seem exasperating and go against one's intuition to use "princess-like handling" with people who themselves turn their backs and do not behave in a constructive manner. It may help to understand that when they were infants, these people never received "princess-like handling" from their parents, so they require it now. One must keep in mind that mentalization can only be learned from the outside in.

For a relationship to develop with someone who does not mentalize and chooses not to enter into a learning relationship, it is important to behave as one would with a toddler and employ the same type of mature and sensitive mind that one would use to teach a child (Midgley & Vrouva, 2012).

Mentalization-based teaching focuses on how natural elements of interaction between a parent and child can be used to develop the child's emotions and his or her ability to mentalize: to do what good parents would do. However, one must in particular apply the pro-development elements of the normal parent-child interaction in terms of developing the child's feelings, and the ability to mentalize, and to support overall positive development. A mother develops the capacity for this interaction over time; through pregnancy, birth, and the first moments with the child (Stern, Bruschweiler-Stern, & Freeland, 1999). The professional has not lived through these phases with the child. It therefore does not come as naturally, so professionals have an extra challenging task that requires continuous training and supervision. There is also a need for a constructive environment, where the mentalizing perspective remains constantly in focus.

The main interest of mentalization-based teaching is what is going on in the child's inner world, and the knowledge that all behaviour is based on the child's feelings, thoughts, and intentions. However, the child's behaviour also affects what others feel and think and, ultimately, how they behave. Therefore, the task is to maintain interaction where mental states are in focus while being aware of the professional's own lack of knowledge of what may be going on in the other person's mind.

To be successful, it is necessary to engage in all interactions with a mentalization stance (Allen, Fonagy, & Bateman, 2010; Bateman & Fonagy, 2007).

The main processing element in mentalization-based teaching and therapy is to meet the client with a stance characterised by an **Open (ÅBENT)** mind.

An Open (ÅBENT) mind

An Open mind (represented by the Danish acronym "ÅBENT"), in this sense, is characterised by the following traits: openness ("**Å**benhed"), balance ("**B**alance"), empathy ("**E**mpati"), curiosity ("**N**ysgerrighed"), and patience ("**T**ålmodighed").

The stance is the "garden" where therapy grows and develops the basis for working with the neglected and traumatised. The Fonagy group views the stance as the central tool in mentalizing treatment.

The stance must reflect an Open mind (Hagelquist, 2012), reflecting: openness, balance, empathy, curiosity, and patience. When working with the neglected and traumatised, it is easy to become involved in conflicts and be overwhelmed by strong emotions like anger or impotence. In those situations, the brain loses its ability for long, complex reflections (Levine, 1998; MacLean, 1990). It is important to create a stance characterised by clear and easily accessible values. Here it is important to remain open-minded. The risk of not maintaining this attitude in conflict situations is precisely what results in targeting behaviour rather than a person's mental state.

Openness demands breaking away from your own preconceptions and being open to the mental states that have led the child at risk to behave in the way in which he is behaving. The professional can express this by listening to the child without judging him, refraining from criticism, and avoiding guessing what the child or adolescent is feeling (Allen, Fonagy, & Bateman, 2010; Bateman & Fonagy, 2007).

In addition, the professional should be aware that the child's unique history is the key to understanding the mental states behind his behaviour. An open stance is an expression of the recognition that mental states are opaque and that it is not possible to have a better idea about what is going on in another person's mind than the person has himself (Allen, Fonagy, & Bateman, 2010).

Balance is significant. Professionals are continually focusing on maintaining a balance. This applies to the four dimensions of mentalization mentioned earlier in this chapter. Neglected and traumatised children and adolescents experience difficulties with the aspect of mentalization that focuses on maintaining a balance between being mindful of themselves and being mindful of others (Allen, Fonagy, & Bateman, 2010). They can become too preoccupied with their own mental states or the other person's mental states – neglected and traumatised children often switch between too much focus on their own mental states and those of others.

Empathy is necessary when trying to put yourself in the vulnerable child's place. Roughly speaking, empathy is "half" of what the mentalization approach is about (Allen, Fonagy, & Bateman, 2010). The shifting of focus used in an empathetic approach, seen in relation to the mentalization approach, can be fruitful in settings in which a professional interacts with children and adolescents. It is by nature an asymmetrical relationship in which the focus should be increasingly placed on the child's mental states rather than the adult's.

Curiosity is necessary when dealing with children who, as a result of the neglect they have suffered, are not often aware of their own internal states. It is also important to remember that the professional does not know more about what the child is thinking than the child himself – in reality, the professional probably knows a lot less (Bateman & Fonagy, 2007, p. 138). The best way to find out how the child or adolescent is experiencing a situation is to be curious and ask them. Sometimes you might be surprised about the answer or think that it simply does not make sense. But being curious can help both yourself and the child reach an understanding that provides a foundation for development.

Patience is absolutely essential when working with children and adolescents at risk. It may often seem like a long road ahead before a child with a history of neglect or trauma can begin to build positive and healthy relationships or find new ways to express his mental states when he interacts with adults. Mentalization-based teaching is a long-term treatment. Child psychiatrist Bruce Perry notes that working with children who have experienced trauma requires two things that are often in short supply in the modern world: time and patience (Perry & Szalavitz, 2011, p. 271). It takes time before these children allow themselves to believe that looking after themselves is not the safest option and that it would be more helpful for them to take the courage to open up and trust people. This is a natural consequence of their experience of being hurt by the people who have first been responsible for looking after them.

All elements of the Open-minded ("ÅBENT") stance are also applicable to the professionals' own mental state. This means that they should also be able to reflect on their own behaviour and be open, balanced, empathetic, curious, and patient in relation to themselves while always remembering that they cannot have a better idea of what is going on in someone's mind than the person does himself.

STORM model, see page 73. The last part of the book is built around this model, so that the processing tools presented in Part 4 all refer to STORM models.

The STORM model

The STORM model consists of an assortment of effective elements from traditional trauma therapy and mentalization-based trauma therapy (Hagelquist, 2012). STORM is an acronym which stands for **S**ecurity, **T**rauma focus, **O**btaining skills, **R**esource focus, and **M**entalization. Incorporating this acronym in your work is a mnemonic (systematic) way to remember the key elements of trauma treatment. The word STORM can also be seen as a symbol of the field you are working in: that is, working with traumatised children, adolescents, and their families. It is a field full of energy and strength. The storm can have a constructive force: cleaning up, initiating development, and creating a balance. But it can also be destructive and dangerous (Hagelquist, 2012).

During a meeting with a neglected and traumatised client, you can easily convince yourself that once this storm passes, everything will be simple. The STORM metaphor can help you remember that this stormy field will generally continue to be so. Imagining a brighter day should not take the focus away from the storm that is raging here and now that may offer a neglected and traumatised patient the opportunity to learn something new – for example, how to be in relationship and to be with others in the midst of a seemingly unbearably emotional place in their life.

Security and mentalization are the first and last elements of the model and, thus, the two elements that frame the model. This is also how it is in practice. Security and mentalization offer an excellent framework for trauma treatment. Without them, the other treatment elements could not be effective. When the child no longer feels safe, or when the treatment is no longer mentalization-based, his feeling of safety should always be restored before the treatment can continue.

The O in the model can be viewed as the eye of the storm and it is here that one operates on obtaining the skills that the child has not yet developed. When working with the neglected and traumatised, focus should be on the eye of the storm – obtaining skills. That's what it says in the action plans. The lack of skills creates difficulties for the child or adolescent in everyday life, that's why you will often be busy building them. The following example describes how paradoxical it can seem to focus on Obtaining skills, when security has not been established.

A woman comes to a psychologist for a third consultation for cognitive behavioural therapy intended to help her develop the skills to regulate her emotions. The woman is weeping hysterically and says that she has just come from a visit to the hospital where she learned that she has advanced and most likely fatal pancreatic cancer. The psychologist tells the woman that it is important that they stick to the manual and that the skills she is obtaining at developing alternative thought processes also will help in her current situation. After handing the woman a tissue, the psychologist asks the woman to find the homework they agreed she would work on at the last consultation so they can get started.

The knowledge that the woman is obviously not calm enough to learn seems to be difficult to relate to working with children and adolescents. Focusing on safety and trauma does not require that you have to give up and not work with these abilities. You just have to have realistic expectations and have no goal other than giving the child a positive experience. No one benefits from being seen as a victim. Establishing a goal of developing unrealistic skills is not appropriate when working with the vulnerable. Working in the field, I see daily how children and adolescents are criticised and punished for not being cooperative and willing to develop skills. This happens despite the fact that they have no sense of security and, for example, do not know where they will be living for the next month or perhaps have parents who are terminally ill, suicidal, violent, sexually abusive, or have some other issue. Likewise, I see that the professionals, who are struggling to provide security for the vulnerable, are subjected to suspicion and criticism when setting cautious, realistic goals for those who are not in secure situations.

Security
Establishing security is about providing a safe living environment for the child, so he can put his energy towards developing rather than just surviving. This applies to both ensuring that he is safe from exposure to new trauma and establishing security in his relationships and environment, just as work needs to be done to establish security in relation to the child's network.

Security, which includes both physical and psychological security, is the basis for ongoing development and trauma processing. Without it, effective treatment would not be possible. Establishing security must come before all other tasks:

"No other aspect of the treatment has a chance of succeeding if no adequate provisions for security are made" (Herman, 1995, p. 196). But there is a tendency to put the steps of developing skills and achieving goals so much too early in focus that they can undermine the value of basic security.

When offering the child security, it is essential to keep his "mind in mind" and be curious and open to what is really going on in his thoughts. A large portion of establishing security is to offer a secure relationship. The starting point for an interaction that promotes development is simply that the child is offered a safe and harmonious relation to a primary caregiver (Bowlby, 1969).

A child's sense of survival has evolved based entirely on his associations. Children who have been in insecure situations have been forced to be more focused on survival, rather than on learning and exploring their own mental states. The idea that vulnerable children need to work with professional adults who do not get involved simply does not apply here. The professional should get involved, always aware of the knowledge that the bond can be broken. Should that happen, it is important to remember that development and experiences can still happen within the context of the break-up by focusing on feelings, needs, goals, and reasons, and creating a new experience by saying a proper goodbye.

In the treatment of children with attachment trauma, it is likely that the subject of security will surface repeatedly. One reason could be that they have had negative relationships with family members who have violated them, or that when they come home to visit their parents, they experience new traumas. Moreover, they are often ill-equipped to look after themselves in relationships – it is often seen, for example, that a young girl who has lived through violence in her childhood finds a violent boyfriend in later life. Every time a child's or adolescent's security is threatened, you must work hard to make sure that they can be safe again.

Establishing security also demands that the child is offered a safe physical environment. The child needs to feel that he is in a safe home where his needs are met and where he feels that he belongs. Creating a framework of care is also significant. Do conversations take place in private? Is the child's individuality reflected in his room? Is it permitted to lock the door of the women's shelter? Proper structuring of the physical setting signals that you are creating an environment of quality, convenience, and worthy of attention (Cameron & Maginn, 2010; Pughe & Philpot, 2007).

A sound sleep is a basic requirement for creating a sense of security. If a child cannot sleep, he is unable to create the sense of calm needed to learn and function optimally. Many neglected and traumatised children have great difficulty sleeping, and it is important to take this seriously. In Part 4, there are a number of ideas for how to work with sleep problems.

Security in the child's network is also important. The people surrounding the child – from school, the parents, grandparents, and caregivers – must work together so that the child can experience a safe and consistent environment. Another way to establish security is to use the model with the angel, to draw an image of good persons from childhood ("angel in the nursery").

In the early part of Part 4 (page 160) there is a checklist for ways to create security.

Trauma focus

The education staff working with traumatised children are advised to have a fundamental knowledge of the impact of trauma on children when trying to understand children's behaviour, to "trauma focus". Trauma has a major impact on the thoughts that go through a child's mind, as trauma colours the mind in a way that no other experience can.

It cannot be stressed enough how important it is that professionals working with traumatised people know as much as possible about trauma and post-traumatic responses (see Hagelquist, 2012 for a thorough review of trauma and the reactions to it). It is also an important part of the treatment of traumatised children for the child to acquire common knowledge about trauma reactions (psychoeducation). When the child hears about these normal reactions, he will realise that he is not alone and that he is not going insane, and that post-traumatic reactions are normal human reactions to extreme circumstances. In addition, it is important for the child to know that it is a condition that can change and that he will be able to heal again (Herman, 1995). This is illustrated in the two following examples:

> A woman lost her infant daughter twelve years ago. For ten years, she was awakened every night by the sound of her late daughter crying. She decided two years ago to understand the loss of her daughter as a trauma and that the sound of the child's crying was the reliving of that trauma. The woman managed to bury the little girl's ghost in her mind by reviewing her daughter's medical records and keeping a journal about the experience. Since then, the woman has been able to sleep through the night. The "mental funeral" of her daughter has brought her peace.

A man spoke about his otherwise healthy son who becomes extremely upset and completely uncontrollable if someone beats repeatedly against something or knocks on anything so that it makes a sound. The father and his son then recalled that when the boy was in an incubator, the nurses would tap on the glass before taking blood samples. They understand that the sound triggers memories of the painful treatments that occurred while the son was in the incubator.

These examples illustrate how important it is to understand trauma and the reactions to it. The professional may also try to help the network around the traumatised child understand and learn to view reactions as a post-traumatic response.

This book places a strong emphasis on trauma. Part 2 deals with psycho-education, and includes PTSD diagnosis, developing trauma diagnosis, and a number of models of how the traumatised brain works. In Part 4, the STORM model is used to show a number of tools that can be used in the treatment of trauma. It is important to remember that it is possible to work with traumatic triggers (page 175), 90/10 responses (page 177), and genesis (page 183) without knowing everything about the original trauma. A trauma sufferer's limits have been exceeded, so it is important that a professional dealing with them does not – whether in conversation, via signals, or through emotional displays – cross those limits once again. It is a delicate balance that requires mentalization.

Obtaining skills – the eye of the storm
Obtaining skills refers to giving the child support in obtaining skills that he has not developed sufficiently because he has lived a life focused on survival rather than development.

It is difficult to help neglected and traumatised children and adolescents build new skills. These children are often *asymmetrically* developed as a result of their upbringing. In some areas they have developed chronologically according to their biological age, whereas in other areas they are much younger. This is due to the trauma they have experienced, often repeatedly, at the hands of their primary caregivers during their development (D'Andrea, Stolbach, Ford, Spinazzola, & van der Kolk, 2012; van der Kolk, 2005a, 2005b). As a result, they use their energy to survive rather than to develop. This has implications for the extent to which they learn how to regulate important developmental domains.

Children living in normal developmental interaction with their caregivers evolve and learn how to regulate themselves from within. The six developmental domains in which they build skills are related to: behaviour, emotions, physique, cognition/attention, their sense of self, and relationships. The vulnerable child may be well developed in some of the domains in accordance with his age because he has certain skills in these domains or because there has been a particular emphasis on supporting the child in regulating the domains. In other domains, the child may operate far below his age level. These children are not only asymmetrically developed, they may actually function differently within the same domain depending on the pressure placed on them in different circumstances.

This can be expressed as follows:

> The challenge is that, in one moment, you will need to have expectations and provide experiences that are appropriate for a five year old, for example, when you are teaching him a specific cognitive concept. Ten minutes later however, the expectation and challenges will have to match those for a younger child, for example, when you are trying to teach him to interact socially. He is developmentally a moving target. This is why parenting these children is such a frustrating experience. One moment you are doing the correct thing, and the next, you are out of sync. (Perry & Szalavitz, 2011, p. 223)

The description is very applicable to situations professionals face when they are working with children who have developed asymmetrically. The key to helping them grow is to understand where they are developmentally – not what their age-appropriate skills should be. Work on building the children's skills must be relevant to their level of development, but you must also give them some challenges so they can be rewarded for their achievements.

On page 77, there is a model for obtaining skills where you can analyse the child's developmental age.

Emotions and behaviour
I will briefly highlight two of the domains used in building skills: emotions and behaviour. Emotions, because they are central to mentalization-based treatment and behaviour because it is an area that I have done much work in lately.

Many neglected and traumatised children experience clear difficulties in detecting their emotions, categorising them, and articulating them. The most likely reason is that there has been little space for negative emotions in their childhood homes. Most parents know how to handle their child's joy and happiness, but often they have difficulty coping with his fear, anger, sadness, or disgust. This means that the child does not develop a sufficient understanding of these emotions (Allen, Fonagy, & Bateman, 2010; Dunn & Brown, 2001). To reach an optimal understanding of their own emotions, parents should have a general awareness of emotions and should consider negative emotions as an opportunity to teach their children something (Gottman, Katz, & Hooven, 1996).

Being able to detect, categorise, and articulate emotions lay the foundation for one's ability to regulate emotions, mentalize, and take personal decisions.

In order to be able to support a child in detecting, categorising, and articulating his emotions, there needs to be a common agenda that defines the meaning of different emotions. This guide therefore offers a wide range of processing tools that can be used to support efforts to detect, categorise, and verbalise emotional states.

It is, however, important to be aware that it is often easier for children to detect, categorise, and articulate feelings when there is no direct eye contact, when they look at something else. It may be when the child is a passenger in the car, when going for a walk, when peeling potatoes, or when it is otherwise occupied. In these situations moments of presence may arise where the child can verbalise his inner life.

When using the tools, the caregiver must be very careful about teaching a child about his own mental states. It is seen all too often that children who have spent many years in an educational framework have overtly taken on "pedagogical parrot speak", which has no association with reality but is rather an echo of the previous caregiver's moral admonitions.

> The problem with this type of artificial "pedagogical parrot speak" is that it has no depth. It has no connection with earlier self-representations, it is not consistent with emotional experience and will therefore be unable to stimulate his or her own mentalization process. Therefore, this kind of understanding is superficial in relation to the inner world, and the patient cannot use it in the everyday mosaic of unpredictable interpersonal events (Karterud & Bateman, 2011, p. 49).

Behaviour domain

When I started teaching mentalization, I often said that behaviour was the last domain that should be addressed because the child or adolescent often first needed to develop the other domains that are the basis for regulating behaviour. One example is to work with the ability to regulate emotions before attempting to regulate behaviour during outbursts of rage. However, I have experienced that even those centres that work professionally and consistently with mentalization often express frustration over the lack of regulation of behaviour. One educator said, "We have become so mentalized that we do not dare say anything when we see unfair behaviour. That leads to our own limits being exceeded and that doesn't work for me." This is not a good situation either for the professional or for the neglected and traumatised children who need to be in consistent environments where they experience structure and daily routines.

Therefore, it is important for me to emphasise that mentalization does not contradict the more common types of behavioural regulation. You can see it as a balancing act between flexibility, chaos, and mentalization on the one hand and strict borders and behaviour control on the other. The illustration shown at page 135 was inspired by Siegel & Bryson (2014) and it shows that one should navigate to stay in the middle of the river and not embrace chaos and only focus on mental states, nor should one be overly rigid and focused on behaviour.

Articulating and regulating inappropriate behaviour is a natural part of creating a view and structure of the lives of neglected and traumatised children. Using mentalization in regulating inappropriate behaviour helps you to regulate emotions, understanding one's own and the child's mental states, and then regulate behaviour from a more reflective perspective.

Resources
Neglected and traumatised children have often experienced hearing themselves being described in negative terms and they have seldom had the positive feeling of being proactive in their own lives. When you work with them to help them identify their own resources it gives them a more positive self-perception, gives them a purpose, and helps them to uncover their potential. In this context, the word "resources" can be understood quite broadly. It can refer to natural talents, qualities, personal characteristics, and coping mechanisms.

By focusing on children's resources, it is possible to identify the traits that got them through the trauma they experienced and to see what they are doing to regain stability in their lives. When working with traumatised children, it can be an effective approach to do what the professionals have done – working specifically to clarify what their resources are. Professionals who work with traumatised children find that most of the time is occupied by everyday activities. In relation to education, requirements for traumatised children are often similar to the expectations of a normal school situation (Bloom, 2005). Within everyday contexts with common expectations, the risk is that the focus will largely be on negative behaviours, easily overlooking the child's resources. In order to empower the child and offer positive development, it is important to keep the focus on the child's resources. Part 4 offers a number of tools for working with resources.

Maintaining mentalization
Trying to maintain a mentalizing outlook when interacting with children and adolescents who have not developed particularly sound mentalization techniques can be difficult. The Fonagy group says that mentalization care environments are characterised by being "… flexible in their thinking and not locked onto

I have found it very important to highlight the natural behavioural strategies in Part 4 (pages 213–223). There are also several models on these pages that show how to work with behaviour proactively and by using mentalization rather than being reactive and punitive.

a particular point of view. They have a playful approach and use warm humour. Problem solving takes place as a process of give and take with respect for each other's views" (Allen and others in Sorensen, 2009, p. 418). This is also reflected in the use of mentalization language, "that is open and respectful and which reflects a reasonable due diligence not to overestimate the limits of one's knowledge about others' mental states" (Allen and others in Sorensen, 2009, p. 418).

An important part of instilling a culture of mentalization in an educational setting is being aware of how you identify, highlight, and praise good examples of mentalization. In residential institutions or in foster families there should always be an awareness of how mentalization is expressed in daily interaction. When they observe mentalization being carried out, the caregivers should draw attention to how impressive and meaningful it is (Hagelquist, 2012). Mentalization fosters mentalization, and this should be seen in all the areas surrounding neglected and traumatised children.

The intervention spectrum

One of the main elements of mentalization-based therapy is the intervention spectrum (Bateman & Fonagy, 2007). It can not only be used in therapy, but is also very useful in teaching and in analysis of where interventions should be used.

The reason that it seems so useful is that the model focuses on the essence of mentalization: that we are unable to mentalize when we are experiencing intense emotions. In recent years, the intervention spectrum has been modified and simplified by the Fonagy group. This book contains the most recent version (Fonagy & Allison, 2014). The concept of the intervention spectrum remains the same. Treatment strategies are constantly moving back and forth within the spectrum, based on emotional intensity and the capacity to mentalize. When emotions are running high, the ability to mentalize is diminished, and vice versa. Professionals using mentalization constantly monitor the intensity of the emotions of adolescents and adapt their treatment (Allen, Fonagy, & Bateman, 2010, p. 213).

See the model of the intervention spectrum on page 79.

As stated, the intensity of emotion is the focus of the spectrum. As emotional intensity increases, the ability to mentalize is diminished. Supportive and empathetic interventions are what are required in those situations. Once the capacity to mentalize has been stabilised, work can begin on interventions at a higher level within the spectrum.

Fonagy and his colleagues say that you cannot strike while the iron is hot. When emotional levels are high, the capacity to mentalize is reduced. "We reflect on everything with greater clarity when we are looking back, than when we are in the midst of a turbulent emotional interaction …" (Bateman & Fonagy, 2007, pp. 155f.). When the iron is hot, it is only possible to work within that part of the spectrum consisting of empathy and support. Once emotions are stabilised, it is possible to move into higher levels of the intervention spectrum.

It is also recommended that you do not attempt to "strike while the iron is too cold". Adolescents need to learn to develop mentalization skills while feeling intense emotion so as to be able to understand the different facets of relationships as they are unfolding (Allen, Fonagy, & Bateman, 2010; Bateman & Fonagy, 2007). Parenthetically, it can be said that it is not always necessary to experiment with mentalization training in a teaching context. Rather, efforts can be directed at reducing the emotional intensity so that the adolescent can be included in the instructional context, take part in an educational opportunity, or simply calm down.

A conversation moves up and down the intervention spectrum solely based on the level of emotional intensity and mentalization capacity. The conversation should always start at giving the person with whom you are working support and empathy. Adolescents can be challenged during the conversation, but if they become overwhelmed by emotions, the professional should revert to a supportive and empathetic attitude. Movements within the spectrum must go slowly, and if the professional has any doubt, it is preferable to be in the supportive and empathetic region and avoid challenging the adolescent's perceptions (Allen, Fonagy, & Bateman, 2010).

The next example shows what happens when the intervention spectrum is *not* used in a teaching situation:

A young girl sitting at the breakfast table in an institution angrily shouts, "I think it's been a shitty fucking morning, and I hate getting out of bed when Mette is the one that wakes me!" The teacher, who is also at the table, replies, "Mette is a sweet girl. What is this nonsense?" The young girl pushes her chair back and slams up to her room.

Let's see what might have happened if the teacher had worked with the girl using the intervention spectrum.

Support and empathy
In the supportive and empathetic section of the spectrum, the professional is welcoming, respectful, and positive about what the adolescent is saying. The caregiver's enquiries are interested and open. Through his attitude, the caregiver communicates that he wants to understand. He does not display an "all-knowing" attitude, and makes sure that he truly understands what he is hearing. The professional can expand the emotional content of the story away from traditional psychology and knowledge (Bateman & Fonagy, 2007). The example of the young

woman that was unhappy by being awakened by the social worker Mette might instead look like this:

> When the young girl says, "I think it's been a shitty fucking morning, and I hate getting out of bed when Mette is the one that wakes me!", it is obvious that her emotions are running high. The teacher must be supportive and empathetic and could say, for example, "I also have a hard time with mornings, and I always say that if I am not awakened just right, I feel like I've got up on the wrong side of the bed. Is that how you feel?"

Exploration

The next phase of the intervention spectrum is exploration. It is about making sense of the behaviour and putting it into context through mentalization (Bateman & Fonagy, 2007, p. 170). The professional should work with the adolescent to gain an overview of the feelings that led to the breakdown of mentalization and the behaviour that resulted from that failure. The session rewinds to the events that led up to the present moment. The professional guides the adolescent back to the moment directly before the breakdown of mentalization, and focuses on the feelings that disturbed the process. By recognising the emotions at stake, and understanding how they came about, it is possible to reduce the adolescent's confusion and provide the proper support for mentalization. It is also important to understand the historical background of emotional reactions, especially seemingly disproportionate reactions. During the exploration phase, it is not the intent to mentalize behaviour.

Exploration might have created the following dialogue:

> When the young girl was a bit more relaxed and had had time to butter her morning roll, the teacher could have asked, "Explain what was so annoying about this morning. What happened? It sounded like there was something about the way you were awakened that made you angry and upset." The girl replies, "It's Mette. She comes in so fast, stomping around in her high heels, just like my mother did." The teacher then asks, "So the high heels perhaps make you frightened or angry?"

Basal mentalization

The third part of the intervention spectrum works directly with mentalization. The rewind method is also used here, but it examines what happened from a mentalization perspective. The professional now attempts during the conversation to restore the mentalization process. The long range goal is to establish a robust and flexible mentalization environment that is impervious to intense emotional states (Bateman & Fonagy, 2007, pp. 179f.).

The young girl is sitting quite calmly and eating her morning roll. The teacher says, "So, a lot happens inside you when you wake up to the sound of high heels. Why do you think Mette is in such a hurry in the morning?" The girl replies, "I think she is stressed and worried that we won't get to school on time." The teacher praises the young girl for being so good at putting herself in the other person's place and says, "That seems likely. I often feel the same way when I have to wake you up."

Mentalizing the relation

In the fourth and final step of the intervention spectrum, mentalization focuses on relationships that the adolescent is currently a part of, including the relationship with the caregiver.

The aim is to get the adolescent to focus on another person's mental state. By using the relationship, it is possible to show that the same behaviour can be experienced differently by different people.

Bateman and Fonagy (2007, p. 192) emphasise that this is a cooperation where it is the journey, not the goal, that is important. They use the image of a professional and adolescent sitting next to each other and examining the adolescent's thoughts and feelings. Together they are concerned with how the mind works:

The teacher asks, "What do you think of this conversation?" The adolescent responds, "I know you hate it when I talk about other staff members, and that you think that I'm negative towards everything and everyone." The teacher responds, "It is true that I find it a little difficult to talk about my colleagues, but I think it is important to understand what is going on inside you, and I really do not think you are negative about everything."

In this example, the adolescent moves directly down through the spectrum. It is far more common that the level of intensity oscillates back and forth, and that the professional, as a result, also moves back and forth in the spectrum, depending on the level of emotional intensity. When conversations or interactions feel stagnant, it is always a good idea to examine the intervention spectrum and check whether the conversation has moved too far and too fast down the spectrum.

Natural developmental interactions

The penultimate model that I will introduce in this refresher chapter includes the basic elements of the natural developmental interactions between a parent and child. This model is central to the theory of mentalization and is also effective in the analysis of treatment. Additionally, the model focuses on how vital it is that the professional is able to reflect on her own needs and create her own sense of inner peace. This is underscored by the fact that Part 3 of the book deals only with professional reflection and mentalization ability.

In the natural developmental interaction between parent and child, the child learns how to regulate his emotions through a communication system consisting of three elements: recognition, reflection, and marked mirroring. The mother can recognise the child's emotions, then reflect upon them in her own mind before returning them in a mirrored form. In this type of interaction, it is possible to regulate the child's feelings in the same way as you turn the volume up or down on a stereo. This communication can be transferred directly to the work of developing children's and adolescents' abilities to regulate their emotions.

It can also be used to understand the difficulties that have occurred in the child's primary care environment by looking at differing mirroring styles (see page 84).

In the three examples below, we look at the two types of mirroring styles and natural developmental interactions which are often encountered in professional work. The examples concern a foster mother caring for a seven-year-old boy. The boy spends every second Sunday at his biological mother's apartment. The mother is young, and things do not always go well when the two are together. The boy seems insecure and a bit frightened when saying goodbye to the foster mother.

The foster mother overreacts to the situation

The foster mother feels and recognises the boy's fear, but fails to reflect and regulate her own anxiety. She reflects to the boy a sense of anxiety of the same intensity as his own – this is not "marked mirroring". The foster child can feel that his foster mother is frightened, which does not help him categorise, articulate, and regulate his own anxiety.

The foster mother's response may create an alien self

The foster mother misinterprets the boy's anxiety and confuses it with anger. She reflects the anger and offers a marked mirroring and says, "You have a right to be angry about having to visit your mother." Her inappropriate response causes the boy to confuse his anxiety with anger. He now believes that her marked mirroring reflects the anxiety he is experiencing and learns to label anxiety as anger. Repeated over and over, this will cause the boy to confuse his own fear with anger. Since the mirroring is flawed, he will be unable to see himself, and the alien self will distort and divide his self-image.

> **Development promoting interaction**
> The foster mother recognises the boy's anxiety. She reflects on her own concerns
> and anxieties but separates them from the boy's. She creates a marked mirror that
> reflects uncertainty but also works to reduce it. The boy learns the correct label for
> anxiety and the foster mother supports him in regulating the emotion.

The end of Part 1 offers a number of models that can be used to explore the child's care environment as to what type of neglect the child may have been exposed. There are lists of the symptoms of the various forms of neglect, such as sexual abuse and violence. There is also a model illustrating the different types of attachment patterns.

The integrated model – the building blocks of mentalization in teaching and therapy

This section provides a model that integrates the key major concepts used in the mentalization-based treatment of neglected and traumatised children and adolescents. The model shows that having an Open (ÅBENT) mind is seen as the basis for treatment. The treatment consists of the STORM model on the one hand and the intervention spectrum on the other. Together, they form the framework for treatment.

Using the intervention spectrum and STORM model requires that they are both used to monitor the client's safety and emotional state. Establishing security must come before all other tasks, and if emotions are running high, treatment should begin with empathy and support.

At the centre of the model lies the "eye of the storm", which is made up of a number of building blocks. These are the skills to be developed through treatment. The idea of this guide is to present the models that support the integrated model and offer practical tools to build mentalization skills in the eye of the storm.

The building blocks of mentalization

The STORM Model

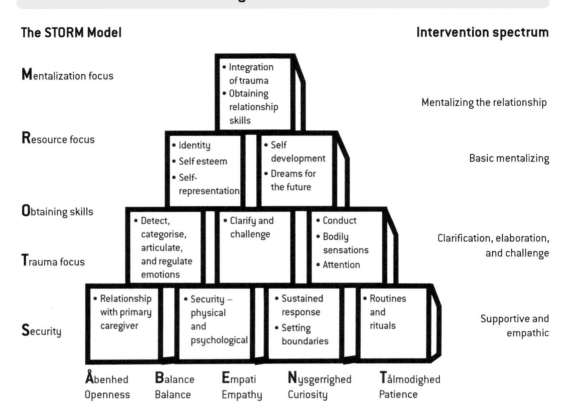

Mentalization focus

- Integration of trauma
- Obtaining relationship skills

Resource focus

- Identity
- Self esteem
- Self-representation

- Self development
- Dreams for the future

Obtaining skills

- Detect, categorise, articulate, and regulate emotions

- Clarify and challenge

- Conduct
- Bodily sensations
- Attention

Trauma focus

Security

- Relationship with primary caregiver

- Security – physical and psychological

- Sustained response
- Setting boundaries

- Routines and rituals

Åbenhed
Openness

Balance
Balance

Empati
Empathy

Nysgerrighed
Curiosity

Tålmodighed
Patience

Intervention spectrum

Mentalizing the relationship

Basic mentalizing

Clarification, elaboration, and challenge

Supportive and empathic

Note: The model is developed in collaboration with psychologist Line Sangild Thimmer – an employee of the Center for Mentalization.

The concept of this book is to support professional work with models and tools. The remainder of the book consists of four parts with associated models and descriptions:

1. **Analysis and theory**: Use the models in this part to create an overview of essential concepts and tools in mentalization-based teaching and therapy.

2. **Psycho-education** (or education of families, children, and adolescents): The models in this section help the child/youth and family better understand themselves and each other. There is particular emphasis on explanation of mentalization and the impact of trauma on behaviour.

3. **Tools for self-reflection**: Exercises for the professional. The professional herself is an important tool in mentalization-based treatment, and therefore should continue to work to develop her own mentalization abilities to create inner peace and make reflexive choices. This is a central part of the guide.

4. **Exercises** to help the caregiver work with the child/adolescent and the family.

Part 1

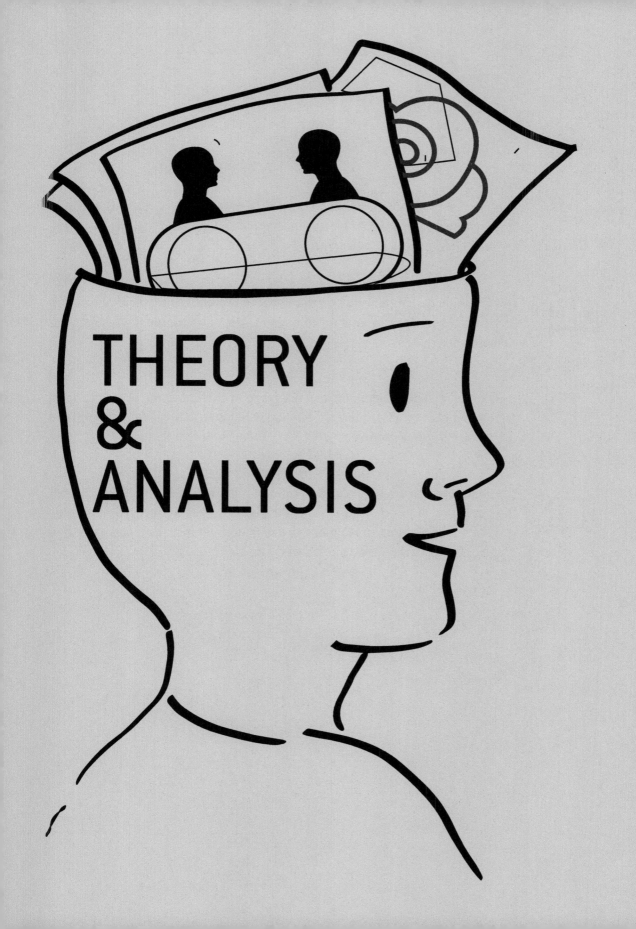

This section presents the essential concepts and tools of mentalization-based treatment that can be used for analysis and a conceptual framework in working with children and adolescents.

METHOD WHAT TO DO

Use the individual models to create an overview of the theory of mentalization and who it concerns in relation to neglect and trauma among children and adolescents.

TIPS AND TRICKS

It is useful for a professional to use the guide to analyse some of the children, adolescents, or families they are already working with to quickly understand how it works and become accustomed to using it as an analytical tool.

EXAMPLE

A psychologist at a residential institution uses models from the first part of the guide one autumn to work with all the adolescents at the institution. This gives the staff a common language to use in understanding adolescents, and some clues as to what they should work on.

Mentalization

Mentalization is a mental activity, concerned with perceiving and understanding one's own behaviour and the behaviour of others based on mental conditions or states.

Mental conditions include feelings, needs, goals, intentions, etc. Peter Fonagy and a wide range of colleagues have over the last decades developed processing models where using mentalization is the central focus.

Mentalization is especially suited for working with vulnerable children and adolescents because it offers a comprehensive theory of the child's development, and a description of the implications of children experiencing trauma and neglect during their development. One of the benefits of using mentalization is that it is an ability that can be learned. This offers positive expectations for development possibilities to traumatised and neglected children and adolescents. In brief, mentalization can be defined this way:

- Mentalization is "holding the mind in mind".
- Mentalization is seeing yourself from the outside and the other person from the inside.
- Mentalization is to have focus on both your own mental state and the mental state of the child or adolescent.
- Mentalization is learning to understand misunderstandings.
- Mentalization is looking beyond the child's behaviour.

What to do?

On the surface, mentalization appears to be an obvious and simple concept. However, often when working with the concept, it is sometimes difficult to understand and maintain the meaning of the term. The model on the next page will help create an image of what mentalization is.

Tips and tricks

It is important to remember that the model is simplified and that mentalization is about a better understanding of your own mental state and that of others. Simply stated, the mental states of everyone involved in the situation are important.

Example

A foster mother is very good at recognising the mental state of the children under the care of herself and their foster father, but she is not tuned in to the mental state of the children's biological mother. The biological mother feels left out and therefore complicates the children's relationship with their new foster family.

MODEL **MENTALIZATION**

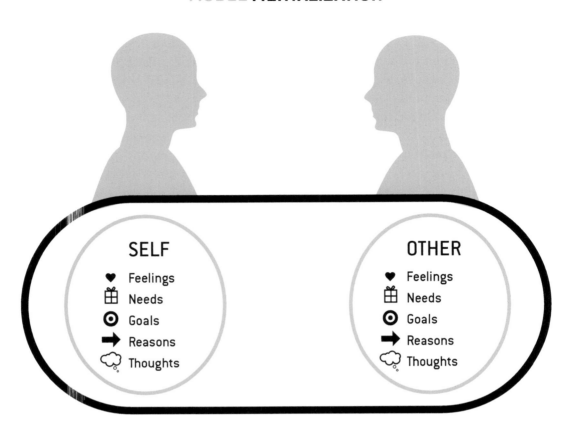

Balancing between the dimensions of mentalization

Balance is key when working with vulnerable children and adolescents. Neglected children and adolescents are experiencing an imbalance in, among other areas, their nervous system (Herman, 1995, p. 63). Further they have difficulties with mentalization, which deals precisely with the ability to balance between being in your own and the other's mind (Allen, Fonagy, & Bateman, 2010). In mentalization you balance between 4 different dimensions. If there is an imbalance it is important to work for a secure new balance.

The four dimensions of mentalization
1. Automatic/implicit as opposed to controlled/explicit
2. Self oriented/other oriented
3. Emotions as opposed to cognition
4. Internally focused/externally focused

What to do?
Assess the balance between the four dimensions.

Tips and tricks
An assessment of the balance sheet is crucial and should give clues on how to correct an imbalance in mentalization. When the adolescent is polarised in one dimension, it is not always possible to address this explicitly. It is important to remember, however, to maintain internal balance, if pointing it out would seem provocative and weaken the mentalization process.

Example
A eighteen-year-old girl says: "I love my boyfriend, and want to do everything to see that he can get a motorcycle when he comes out of prison, so I'd like to have my children's savings account." She stares insistently at the psychologist and says: "Isn't love more important than common sense?" Her psychologist is aware of the imbalance between feelings and cognition, and is at first careful about discussing the subject.

MODEL DIMENSIONS OF MENTALIZATION

Self   Other

Emotions   Cognition

Internally   Externally

Automatic/implicit   Controlled/explicit

Self Focus on own mental state.	**Other** Focus on other's mental state.

Balanced: Being simultaneously aware of your own mental state and the mental state of others.

Unbalanced: Mainly focused on your own mental state or the mental state of others.

Feelings Focus on feelings, desires, needs, and other emotion-based mental states.	**Cognition** Focus on assumptions, thoughts, goals, and other cognitive mental states.

Balanced: Focus on both cognitive and emotion-based mental states.

Unbalanced: When cognitive aspects are ignored and there is excessive focus on emotional states, or when there is too much focus on the cognitive and not enough on the emotional.

Internally focused
Focus on internal conditions of the person or those of others such as intuition.

Externally focused
Focus on external factors such as facial expressions.

Balanced: Focus on both internal and external conditions and circumstances.

Unbalanced: When external circumstances take on too much importance, and internal modes are ignored, the external can be misinterpreted, for example: "He didn't smile when he said hello because he hates me."

Automatic/implicit
Automatic mentalizing is what we do when we are together and automatically seem to understand each other.
Reflexive, quick, and not deliberate.

Controlled/explicit
Controlled mentalizing is what we do when the other person's behaviour no longer seems to make sense and we try to figure out the reasons for their actions. It is a relatively slow process requiring conversation, reflection, and an active mental effort.

Balanced: There is a shift from automatic to controlled mentalization when misunderstandings or conflicts occur, or when you wonder what is happening within the interaction. One switches to controlled mentalization to understand the situation in the light of the current mental conditions.

Unbalanced: Occurs when you exclusively use automatic, simplistic, and distorted assumptions about yourself and the other person, making it hard to challenge them. When emotions are high, automatic mentalization dominates. Imbalance can also occur via controlled mentalization: "She is manipulative, because she suffers from a disrupted attachment pattern" and sees everything through that lens.

With inspiration from Bateman & Fonagy, 2012.

Mentalization failure

Mentalization failure occurs when one is no longer able to focus on one's own mental state or that of the other person. One looses track of both one's own feelings, needs, goals, and reasons, and those of the other person. The ability to mentalize can fail due to intense emotional arousal or a perceived threat (Bateman & Fonagy, 2007). Everyone can find themselves in situations where they lose track of their own and the other's mind. Mentalization failure typically occurs in situations where the subject is experiencing high emotional intensity.

What to do?
Mentalization failure is damaging to our own self-awareness, emotions, and our relationships with others. It is important to analyse what has triggered the failure.

Tips and tricks
View a failure of mentalization as interesting as well as an opportunity to more completely learn something about the child and ways he can be supported. Child psychologist Margaret Blaustein said: "A large display of temper can be regarded as a window to inner development. It is therefore more problematic when these children are overly compliant" (Blaustein et al., 2006). While a failure of mentalization is ongoing, there is a high probability that the professionals involved are experiencing intense emotions, so their ability to mentalize effectively might be impaired. No analysis should be done when emotions are high and when mentalization is failing. The model is a good way to talk about one's own destructive behaviour in a more objective and detached way, as it is generally embarrassing for everyone to discuss a mentalization failure.

Example
A thirteen-year-old boy is hanging out with some older boys, and his foster parents are worried about him getting involved with drugs and crime. When they tell him that they do not want him to spend time with the boys in the city, he throws a tantrum and bites his foster mother on the arm. The parents discuss the situation using the frames of the model. What triggered the boy? What resulted in the mentalization failure? If the foster parents had backed up a little when he was disappointed and angry and let him recover a bit before speaking to him, the situation could have been different. The foster parents follow the model when they speak with the boy about the incident. Using the model, they can speak more constructively about what happened, and give the boy a chance to apologise.

MODEL **MENTALIZATION FAILURE**

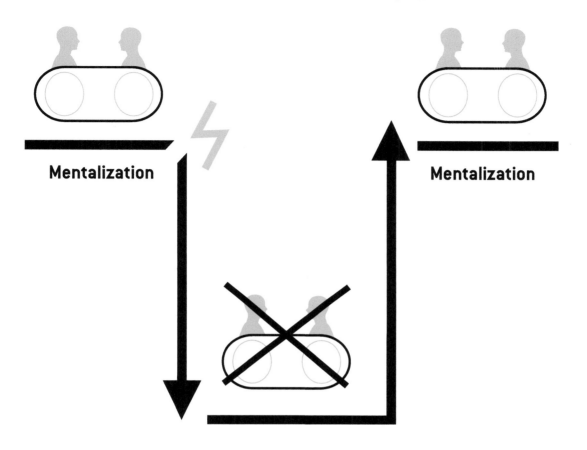

Mentalizing failure – early forms of mentalization

There are three different types of mentalization failure, which reveal themselves in early forms of mentalization – also called pre-mentalization modes (Bateman & Fonagy, 2012):

1. Teleological mode
2. Psychic equivalence mode
3. Pretend mode

These modes concern ways of thinking and interacting that precede mentalization developmentally. It is relevant to know about mentalization failure and pre-mentalization modes in order to be more aware when they arise in oneself and in others.

What to do?

The type of mentalization failure can be determined through conversation or analysis.

Tips and tricks

When the conversation is no longer mentalized, one can stop and examine the feelings present directly before mentalization collapsed.

Example

A mother living in an abusive relationship discusses the violence with a psychologist. She says: "I know it's not good for my children and I want to change my life." She continues to talk and talk. Initially, it seems as if she has obtained new insights, but the psychologist views it as if the woman is a needle on a record player that has become stuck in the same groove, which means that the mentalizing process is stuck in pretend mode. The psychologist tells the mother how unhappy she would be if her relationship with her children's father devolved into serious violence. The woman is touched, the conversation becomes more honest, and the woman reveals her fear of being alone.

Teleological mode	Mental states are expressed in targeted actions rather than through words or thoughts. For example, self-harm is used as a way to communicate extreme pain. Only the physical world matters, for example, "I can only tell that I am sorry when I see blood flowing." Relationships with others are also judged based on external actions, such as "You did not give me a hug, so you must not like me."

Psychic equivalency mode	In this mode, an equivalency is created between reality and mental states. The feeling that mental states are representations is missing and no major difference between reality and fantasy is observed. Examples are dreams, post-traumatic flashbacks, or paranoid delusions. An example of mental equivalency can be seen in statements like, "What I am thinking is reality," "Whatever I think and feel is real. That's how it is." The mode can also be seen in broad and general categorisations like: "He's evil," or "she's cute." Alternative perspectives disappear and there is an exaggerated sense of one's own opinions and personal experiences.
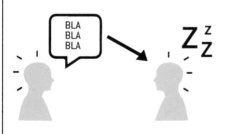	
Pretend mode	In this mode, there is little or no contact between mental states and reality. As opposed to mentalization, mental states are not flexibly related to reality. Pretend mode is seen through pseudo-mentalization, intellectualising, and the use of "psychobabble". There will often be a lack of emotional resonance in the conversation. The content of the speech is exaggerated and uses distorted clichés in a marked manner. Conversation takes on the characteristics of a monologue as the speaker often has no concern as to whether what is being discussed is meaningful to the listener.

Mentalization difficulties

Two forms of inappropriate mentalization are frequently used. They resemble, but indeed are not, mentalizing. The two reviewed here are pseudo-mentalization and the abuse of mentalization (Bateman & Fonagy, 2012).

What to do?

Above all, be aware of inappropriate mentalization in yourself. Pay particular attention to pseudo-mentalization when working with children and adolescents, because it is very easy to become fixated on a certain way of understanding a child or adolescent. This type of pseudo-mentalization can easily affect an entire group of staffers. For example: "She is just manipulative," "Everything is due to her ADHD," "She just wants attention, so do not respond to her self-destructive behaviour."

Tips and tricks

Examine your own tendency for pseudo-mentalization in the exercise "Pseudo-mentalization in practice" (page 152).

Example
A man says to his wife: "I know exactly what you were up to when you came bouncing into the room with your shopping bags while I was watching football. You thought: 'I'll spoil his afternoon so he can sit around and worry about how our finances have been destroyed'" (pseudo-mentalization).

MODEL MENTALIZATION DIFFICULTIES

Pseudo-mentalization	Pseudo-mentalizing sounds like mentalizing because you seem interested when you are discussing another's mental states, but there is a tendency to express certainty without acknowledging the uncertainties associated with knowing about someone's mind – mental states are opaque. There is a fixed idea about what is going on in someone's mind. It can be intrusive (lack of respect for the fact that a mind is individual or opaque – "She's just a classic borderline personality who constantly manipulates") or overactive (trying too hard to understand what others are thinking – "They think that I am embarrassing and that I talk too loud") or destructive (seen in paranoid statements like: "The neighbour is out to bother me by the way he shovels snow").
Abuse of mentalization	The understanding of mental states doesn't fail, but the way in which the understanding is used can be harmful to the other person. This is often seen in the distortion of the other's feelings in order to protect one's own interests. This form of mentalization can be immediately perceived as cognitive empathic understanding, but its aim is to safeguard one's own interests (such as with antisocial personality disorder). The other person's feelings are distorted or exaggerated in order to serve one's own agenda, such as the father who explains his sexual abuse of his own daughter by saying: "She wanted it. Even as a three year old, she was walking around with a bare butt and came into the living room just so I would see her and be turned on."

Assessment of mentalizing ability in adults – a scale of reflexive function

Reflective function (RF) is an operative use of explicit mentalization ability. In the interest of promoting the ability to mentalize to help vulnerable children and their families, it is essential that the treatment and therapeutic approach take place within the zone of proximal development. Often, we as professionals tend to intervene where we would like someone to be, rather than meeting the person where he actually is. Focusing on the level of mentalization can help to ensure that a professional hits the zone of proximal development in a verbal or educational therapy. The measurement of mentalization is difficult when it comes to gathering information about mental states which are not directly observable. Although the measurement of RF has primarily been used in a research context, a professional can still be inspired by the scale, and use it as a kind of map to navigate by in an educational approach or therapy.

What to do?

 RF is commonly assessed using Adult Attachment Interviews (AAI) with challenging questions like: "Overall, how do you think that your experiences with your parents have affected your personality as an adult?" or "Do you think your parents understood that you felt rejected?" The interview questions will inevitably activate the interviewee's type of attachment in the form of feelings and thoughts related to the interviewee's attachment relations. By examining close relationships, it is possible to get an insight into what extent the person will be able to be mentalizing about him- or herself and others when emotions rise. It can be useful to note in what way the person responds to attachment questions and then use the scale to assess the level of mentalization (RF).

Tips and tricks

 RF may be particularly relevant in situations when working with at-risk parents and the relationship with their children.

Example

The mother of an infant goes to a psychologist. According to a parent survey, her mentalization abilities need to be developed, but she is not motivated to change. She says: "I do not understand what they mean. My son is doing well, he smiles when I pick him up, and I dress him in clean clothes every day, so I don't see what I need to change. But the state system is after me because I had harsh words with a stupid social worker. That's why they want to take him from me." With help from the scale, the psychologist is in a position to understand and assist the mother in relation to her limited mentalization abilities.

MODEL SCALE OF REFLEXIVE FUNCTION (RF)

MENTALIZATION LEVEL (RF)		DESCRIPTION	GENERICALLY
Moderate to high RF	9 Complete/ exceptional	The person shows a consistent reflexive attitude in all contexts through an exceptionally advanced mentalization ability which seems genuine, refreshing, surprising, complex, and contextualised in an evolutionary perspective.	**In relation to other people's thoughts and feelings, good mentalization is revealed by:** • That we admit that we often do not know what others think (opacity). • A desire for thought and reflection. • The ability to offer different perspectives. • Sincere interest in other people's thoughts and feelings. • A recognition that mental states are affected by the context and condition in which they are found. • That we can forgive when we understand why the other person acted in a certain manner. **Perception of one's own mental state:** • That one's understanding can change. • Development perspective – that one's understanding of others changes over time (such as the views of one's own parents). • Conflict – awareness of having inconsistent thoughts and feelings. • Curiosity about one's own feelings and thoughts. • Interest in differences, for example, in the way a child's thoughts differ from an adult's. • Awareness of how emotions can distort one's perception of oneself and others.
	7 Significant	The person makes consistent use of a reflexive attitude. There are many examples of full reflexive function that suggest a stable psychological model of his own mental states and the mental states of others. Details concerning the thoughts and feelings and implications of mental states are explicitly stated, and there is a developmental (interactional) perspective.	
	5 Clear/ordinary	The person shows a general ability to understand his own and other people's actions as meaningful based on mental states in the form of, for example, feelings and thoughts. The person has a model of the mind (his own and others), which can be simple, but relatively consistent, personalised, and well-integrated.	

			During conversation, there is no talk about mental states such as feelings, thoughts, or intentions.
Limited to negative RF	3 Questionable/ low	The answers vary in quality. A mentalization perspective is present now and then, but it is inconsistent, and the narrative is filled with social clichés, self-centredness, opinions, an inability to see another's perspective, mixed feelings, conflicts, a lack of development, and a lack of awareness of the mental state's indistinct character. Answers can be affected by "black and white thinking" with a tendency for idealisation and devaluation.	**Answers often have the following characteristics:** • Clichés, trite or superficial considerations. • Excessive detail at the expense of motivation, feelings, or thoughts. • Focusing on outward social conditions, such as school, municipality, neighbours, or government rather than the people involved. • Preoccupation with rules, responsibilities, "should" and "should not". • Denial of involvement in problems. • Reproach or fault-finding. • Lack of acknowledgement of the opaqueness of the mind. • Generalisations and "stuck in their ways". • Tendency to explain behaviour with diagnoses and global personality traits. • Tendency to blame others. • Lack of curiosity concerning the motives of others.
	1 Absent but not defeated	A mentalization perspective is absent in the person, but responses are not actively resistant or hostile. Responses are laced with references to specific events and/or social or psychological clichés that reveal a flawed model of the mind. Most responses are characterised by distortion, and these may seem self-centred in that they are overstated, egocentric, self-aggrandising, or self-congratulatory with unrealistic and/or condescending descriptions of others.	
	-1 Negative	The person appears hostile and resistant to challenging questions and/or responds in a bizarre or contradictory way: "How should I know? Aren't you the psychologist here? You're just trying to bring me down."	

Note: The table was inspired by Karterud & Bateman (2011, pp. 143ff). The table was developed by psychologist Anne Blom Corlin, who is affiliated with the Center for Mentalization.

Mentalization and learning

Mentalization-based therapy and education can be considered a learning relationship. Before the child can be part of a learning relationship, he must have confidence that the other person can teach him something honest and useful. Children who have never been in a positive relationship with an adult can develop a basic distrust of whether adults can teach them something useful about the world. They possibly have never learned to trust anyone but themselves. Other children have experienced that their trust has been abused. They have been taught things about themselves that are simply wrong: for example, the child who has been told that he was "bad" and deserved the violence he endured. These trust issues make it important that a child is convinced that others want to teach him something honest and valuable, and that he will be learning something helpful (epistemic trust). This ability needs to be developed in children who have not learned to trust. If the door to learning is closed, it can only be opened slowly via this and future relationships. Other children have had mixed experiences learning from adults, so with them the door is open sometimes and completely closed at others. Some children are ready to engage in a learning relationship with everyone. They might also do well with computer or net-based therapy and have no need for a personal relationship.

What to do?

Consider the child's basic level of trust in others. If trust is lacking, it must be developed before the door to learning can be opened. A child's trust level can also be volatile. The model offers suggestions on how to proceed depending on the child's level of confidence.

Tips and tricks

The kids who seem the most indifferent and least engaged in learning relationships are often those where intuition tricks the professional into believing that she should start teaching right away – but the child might not be ready to learn. Trust should be the starting point.

Example

A fourteen-year-old boy is part of an immigrant boys group and seems completely indifferent to his contact person. The contact person is worried about the boy, who will soon reach the age of criminal responsibility. The teacher is concerned with everything that he feels he needs to teach the boy, but realizes that he has yet to establish the kind of trust that the boy requires before the door to learning can be opened.

MODEL MENTALIZATION AND LEARNING

Opening the door to learning requires that the child believes the teacher will teach him something positive.

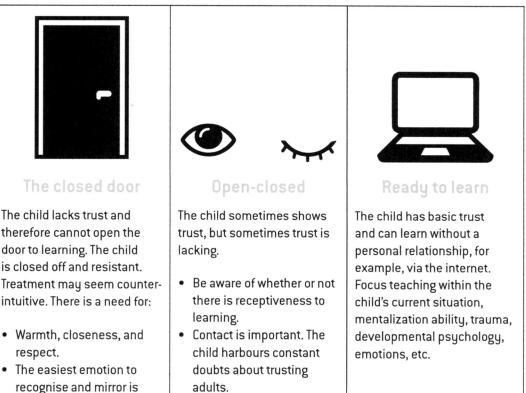

The closed door	Open-closed	Ready to learn
The child lacks trust and therefore cannot open the door to learning. The child is closed off and resistant. Treatment may seem counter-intuitive. There is a need for: • Warmth, closeness, and respect. • The easiest emotion to recognise and mirror is disappointment – "You must have been so disappointed." • A part of the child's development stopped when he decided "No one will ever hurt me again." • Focus on what works. • "Princess instruction."	The child sometimes shows trust, but sometimes trust is lacking. • Be aware of whether or not there is receptiveness to learning. • Contact is important. The child harbours constant doubts about trusting adults. • The relationship requires constant attention for work to continue.	The child has basic trust and can learn without a personal relationship, for example, via the internet. Focus teaching within the child's current situation, mentalization ability, trauma, developmental psychology, emotions, etc.

With inspiration from Fonagy & Allison, 2014; Larson & Maddock, 1995.

Attachment patterns

Around 1970, American psychologist Mary Ainsworth, a student of John Bowlby, developed an experimental procedure to test whether it was possible to measure the quality of a child's attachment to caregivers. That experiment is now one of the most widely used methods for assessing a child's attachment style. In the experiment, Ainsworth examined how children handled both separation from, and reunion with, their mother. This experiment was called "Strange Situation". The experiment showed that children reacted differently depending on their experience of the connection. She deduced and described three attachment patterns. Since then, a fourth attachment pattern has been added.

The following page shows a categorisation of four different types of connections. One should take care, however, not to categorise a person's attachment style from a simple analysis. It should be based on thorough investigation, but the chart does provide an opportunity to reflect on a child's behaviour within its relationships.

What to do?

It might be interesting to do an analysis of what type of attachment the behaviour reflects in order to understand the child's behaviour and be able to be mentalizing in relation to the child.

Tips and tricks

An analysis of attachment patterns requires a thorough test, but it is possible to use the model to develop ideas on understanding a child's behaviour from his attachment experiences.

Example

An eight-year-old girl seems uninterested in her foster parents, despite the fact that she has been in the home for two years. It is helpful for the foster parents to understand that the girl may have developed an insecure and avoidant attachment style as a result of suffering neglect in the past.

MODEL ATTACHMENT PATTERNS

Secure attachment	Experiences the caregiver as a secure base and reacts negatively (e.g., crying) when the caregiver leaves the room. Happy and quickly comforted when she returns. People with secure attachment patterns have a feeling of attachments with people as being available, responsive, and helpful (Bowlby, 1980).
Safe	
Avoidant attachment	Does not respond to caregiver when he is present. When the caregiver leaves, the child does not react and seems equally attached to a stranger as to the caregiver. When the caregiver returns, the child either avoids him or is slow to respond. People with insecure avoidant attachment patterns are not connected to the world in relation to attachments and feel both physically and mentally disconnected (Behrens, Hesse, & Main, 2007).
Avoidant	
Insecure ambivalent	Prior to separation, the child seems insecure and seeks closeness with the caregiver. When the caregiver returns, the child exhibits intense frustration and is very difficult to console. Those with an ambivalent insecure attachment pattern have not succeeded in developing feelings of security in their attachments and, on the one hand, are perceived as possessive, but on the other hand, repelling (Ainsworth & Bell, 1970).
Ambivalent	
Disorganised/ disoriented	The child exhibits a lack of a stable strategy in relating to caregivers by exhibiting a series of confusing and conflicting behavioural traits. People with disorganised attachment patterns lack clear behaviour around their connections. Their actions in relation to connecting with people are often a mixture of avoidance and resistance (Main & Hesse, 1990).
Disorganised	

An Open (ÅBENT) mind

In order to maintain an interaction where mental states remain in focus and ensure that work continues while using the mentalization concept that it is not possible to know what is going on in the other's mind, it is necessary to engage in interactions focused on the mental. When meeting with children and adolescents who have been exposed to neglect and trauma, it is recommended that the approach is based on five concepts: openness ("Åbenhed"), balance ("Balance"), empathy ("Empati"), curiosity ("Nysgerrighed"), and patience ("Tålmodighed"). Together they form the word "OPEN": an open mind (represented by the Danish acronym "ÅBENT") (Allen, Fonagy, & Bateman, 2010; Bateman & Fonagy, 2007).

What to do?

Be aware that the setting is the most difficult, but also the most important part of mentalization-based therapy. The risk of not having the proper setting is the risk of focusing on the child's or adolescent's behaviour rather than his mental state. In mentalization-based treatment, the primary interest should be in what is going on in the child's inner world (Bateman & Fonagy, 2007).

Tips and tricks

Put up a sign saying "OPEN" (ÅBENT) on the refrigerator of your institution or in your home. It may help you to maintain focus when things get difficult.

Example

A pair of foster parents are summoned to a meeting at their foster son's school. They are seated in front of eight professionals from the school, who then tell the parents several things that their son Jonas has told them. Jonas says:

"My foster father tells my foster mother to 'Shut up!'"
"My foster parents have sex while I'm watching."
"I do not think I fit into my foster family."

The foster parents are in shock, but maintain an Open (ÅBENT) mind and try to understand what is going on in Jonas's mind and understand what he may really mean. The foster father remembers that Jonas was very surprised when it dawned on him that the foster parents sometimes shared a blanket. Jonas and his birth mother often watched "Paradise Hotel", and when the people on the programme shared a blanket, it was to have sex. The foster father did once say, "Oh, just shut up" in a playful way to the foster mother, but it was meant as an affectionate joke. Jonas has most likely not experienced that the phrase could be said in jest, and of course misses his mother and believes he would fit better living with her.

MODEL AN OPEN (ÅBENT) MIND

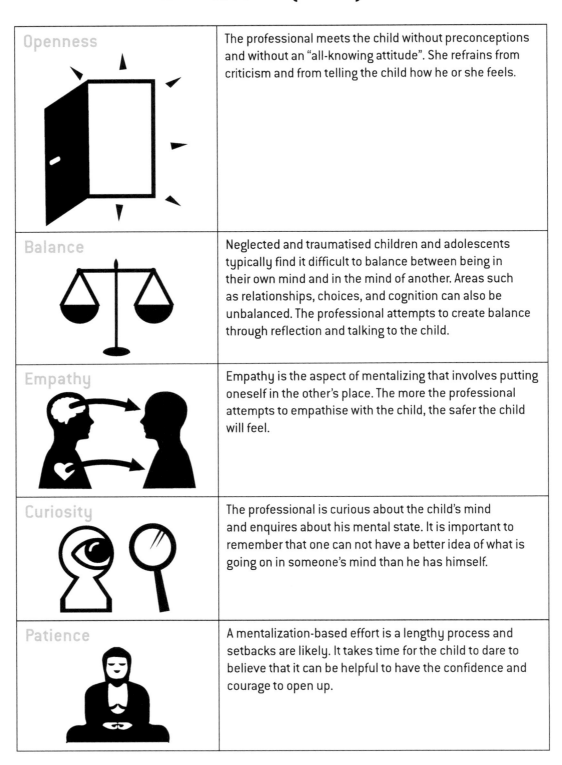

Openness	The professional meets the child without preconceptions and without an "all-knowing attitude". She refrains from criticism and from telling the child how he or she feels.
Balance	Neglected and traumatised children and adolescents typically find it difficult to balance between being in their own mind and in the mind of another. Areas such as relationships, choices, and cognition can also be unbalanced. The professional attempts to create balance through reflection and talking to the child.
Empathy	Empathy is the aspect of mentalizing that involves putting oneself in the other's place. The more the professional attempts to empathise with the child, the safer the child will feel.
Curiosity	The professional is curious about the child's mind and enquires about his mental state. It is important to remember that one can not have a better idea of what is going on in someone's mind than he has himself.
Patience	A mentalization-based effort is a lengthy process and setbacks are likely. It takes time for the child to dare to believe that it can be helpful to have the confidence and courage to open up.

The STORM model

The STORM model consists of a collection of elements from traditional trauma therapy and mentalization-based trauma therapy (Hagelquist, 2012). STORM is an acronym for **S**ecurity, **T**rauma focus, **O**btaining skills, **R**esource focus, and **M**entalization. Incorporating this acronym in your work is a mnemonic (systematic) way to remember the key elements of trauma treatment. The word STORM can also be seen as a symbol of the field you are working in: that is, working with traumatised children and adolescents. It is a field full of energy and strength. The storm can have a constructive force: cleaning up, initiating development, and creating a balance. But it can also be destructive and dangerous (Hagelquist, 2012).

What to do?
Security and mentalization are the first and last elements of the model and, thus, the two elements that frame the model. This is also how it works in practice. Security and mentalization offer an excellent framework for trauma treatment.

Therapists are often preoccupied with building the skills that children and families have not developed sufficiently. While developing skills is a key part of mentalization-based therapy, if a child does not feel secure he will use his resources for protection and pay very little attention to developing new skills.

Tips and tricks
Analyse the child or family using the STORM model. Write the model on the board and discuss how to see the child's overall situation and needs on the basis of the model.

Example

A thirteen-year-old girl with Pakistani roots attends a school for children with emotional difficulties. At school they are aware that work is needed to develop the girl's ability to read others' emotions. She often says to staff: "Don't be angry" or "I can see you're angry with me." Usually, she is misreading their emotions.

The staff have focused on working with material that illustrates emotions and to support the girl's ability to detect and categorise her own emotions, and the emotions of others. Nothing seems to work. After analysing the work with the girl using the STORM model, it suddenly becomes clear to staff that she does not feel safe in her own home. Her father drinks and is often violent. He has told her that he has committed a murder back in Pakistan and that he will kill her if she ever has a Danish boyfriend. The girl secretly has a Danish boyfriend and is always aware of her father's angry looks.

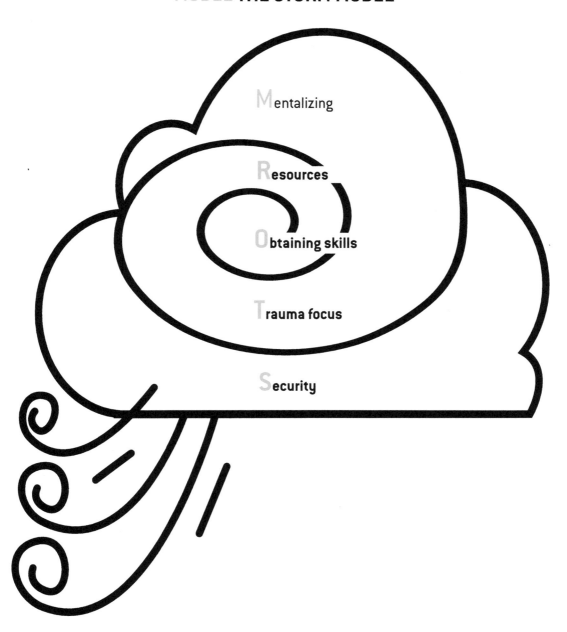

Security

Establishing security is about ensuring that a child is safe from being exposed to new trauma and also about establishing security in his relationships. A sense of security allows the child to put his energy towards developing rather than just surviving. Security is the starting point for any trauma treatment.

Trauma focus

The professionals working with traumatised children are advised to have a fundamental knowledge of the impact of trauma on children. Professionals working with trauma victims should know as much as possible about trauma and post-traumatic responses, also when trying to understand behaviour. The child can be taught about normal reactions to trauma.

Obtaining skills

Obtaining skills refers to giving the child support in building skills that he has not sufficiently developed because he has lived a life focused on survival rather than development. The six development domains are: *emotions, behaviour, attention/ cognition, physique, sense of self, and relationships*. These domains are used to determine the child's current level of development and are discussed in greater detail on the next page.

Resources

Work should assist the child in identifying his own resources in order to give him a more positive self-perception, give him a purpose, and help him to uncover his potential. The professional sees the child's potential and uncovers undeveloped resources. Resources are broadly understood as innate talents, qualities, personal characteristics, and coping strategies.

Mentalization

One should continue mentalizing when meeting with the child, parents, partners, and networks. Moments when mentalizing interactions occur should be praised and highlighted.

Obtaining skills

Part of the STORM model consists of obtaining skills to replace those skills found in developmental trauma disorder. Developmental trauma disorder is a conceptual framework developed by a number of American psychologists (van der Kolk, 2005a, 2005b; van der Kolk et al., 2009) to explain how children and adolescents in upbringing can be preoccupied with survival rather than the development of age-equivalent skills and therefore have typically not developed abilities corresponding to their chronological age.

What to do?

In order to support a child's or adolescent's development, it is crucial to find out where they are in terms of development. The model's six domains can be used to analyse an individual child. Neglected and traumatised children and adolescents are often asymmetrically developed. Efforts should always be adapted to the individual child's level of development in the different areas at different times.

Focus points and objectives can be developed based on an analysis of the six domains.

Tips and tricks

It is important to work with no more than one or two skills at a time. No one can be in development in every area at the same time. Often, the lack of behavioural skills is the most obvious, but behaviour should be viewed as only the top of the pyramid. Other skills must be obtained before the child will be able to change his behaviour.

Example

A foster mother comes in for a consultation. She wants help changing her foster son's behaviour. She feels that her ten-year-old adopted son follows her around the home and never lets her out of sight. The foster father has built a large pirate ship in the garden, because the boy loves pirates. When the foster mother is seated and knitting, the boy immerses himself in books about pirates. Along with the supervisor, an analysis is made of the boy's abilities. It becomes clear that he is completely age-appropriate in relation to cognition and attention, but still reacts as a very young child, who has not yet learned that people still exist when they are out of sight, when it comes to relationships. The foster mother thinks that it is foolish that a child of his age would behave so childishly, but the foster father is more understanding. The next time the boy goes out into the garden, the foster father stands in the living room window and waves as one would to a small child. The boy stays out for over an hour, enjoying some of the wildest pirate adventures to be found on the open seas.

MODEL OBTAINING SKILLS

Write the child's developmental age and chronological age as they relate to the six domains:

	Age	Developmental age
Emotions Able to recognise, categorise, articulate, and regulate emotions. Recognition of the emotions of others.	☐	☐
Behaviour General expectations for behaviour like healthy eating, going shopping, etc. Self-destructive behaviour. Re-enactment of previous trauma. Survival and coping strategies.	☐	☐
Attention/cognition Having age-appropriate skills for sustaining attention and focus in different contexts. Having age-appropriate cognitive functioning. Keeping up in school and possessing general knowledge: who is the president of the United States, etc.	☐	☐
Physical Able to feel cold and warmth. In touch with his body. Able to feel hunger and satiety and able to feel fatigue and to calm himself.	☐	☐
Sense of self Having an experience of a total "Me" (self-representation) – a positive whole self as a result of having been reflected accurately and positively. Experiencing a positive and autonomous sense of "I" (self as an agent): the belief that one can exist positively in the world and succeed in achieving objectives, and that actions and behaviour are recognised and result in the desired outcomes.	☐	☐
Relationships Having close and positive relationships with others, including teachers, a pet, neighbours, family, and others. Equal relationships with peers are important, as is understanding one's role in different relationships. Trust.	☐	☐

The intervention spectrum

One of the main elements of mentalization-based therapy is the intervention spectrum (Bateman & Fonagy, 2007). Treatment strategies constantly move back and forth within the spectrum, based on emotional intensity and the ability to mentalize. When emotions are running high, the ability to mentalize is diminished, and vice versa. Professionals using mentalization constantly monitor the intensity of the emotions of the adolescent they are working with and adapt their treatment (Allen, Fonagy, & Bateman, 2010, p. 213).

What to do?

Focus should be placed on the child's emotional intensity and ability to mentalize rather than on behaviour. When emotional intensity is at its highest one should be aware that the child is in no shape to mentalize and it is necessary to be supportive and understanding. One could say, for example: "I understand that you get angry when you think something is unfair."

Tips and tricks

The intervention spectrum is used in therapy as a teaching tool, but can also be used in difficult discussions, such as at a meeting with parents where the conversation will cause the parents to become emotional. For example, that their child is to be placed in a treatment centre.

Example

The police come out to a man standing on a bridge and threatening to jump. The police negotiator uses the intervention spectrum and determines that the man's emotional intensity is so high that he needs to start out by being "I-supportive". He starts out by saying, "I understand right now that you feel completely lost."

Clarification: "Has something happened that brought you here today?"

Basic mentalizing: "Have you given any thought to coming down? What will this do to your wife and children?"

The man says: "You are just trying to trick me", to which the negotiator responds, "I'm afraid that you will jump, and that will make me sad, but I also know that I can not decide what you will do" (I-supportive). During the process, the negotiator alters the interventions according to the man's emotional intensity. When the man shows intense emotions, the negotiator uses the upper parts of the spectrum. When the man is more calm, the negotiator asks the man how he thinks he will feel if he jumps. When the man is very calm, the negotiator tells the man about people who have survived suicide attempts by jumping off a bridge, who said that after they jumped they regretted it the whole way down (basic mentalization).

MODEL THE INTERVENTION SPECTRUM

Emotional intensity	Mentalizing	
High	Low	Supportive and empathic
		Clarification, elaboration (and challenge)
		Basic mentalizing
Low	High	Mentalizing the relationship

Mentalization in family therapy – MBT-F loop

The MBT-F loop is a central part of mentalization-based family therapy (MBT-F) and it is used at the Anna Freud Centre in London. In family therapy, the loop is used to investigate common interactions within the family, where those interactions are not constructive, due to, among other things, a lack of mentalizing interactions. The loop is a framework that helps health care providers in structuring therapy sessions and work up to mentalized interactions.

What to do?

The model consists of three steps and three "checks".

Step 1. Discovering and naming
The therapist articulates interaction patterns within the family. They then create a common process in which the family works together to study the different interactions. Is it typical? Is it constructive? What happens to whom, and how does it affect the others? The family then is invited to give the patterns a name, such as "shouting mood", "deep silence", or "superficial chatter".

Check: "Does everyone agree that these are the interactions? Is this what you are experiencing in your family?"

Step 2. Mentalize the moment
Mentalize the pattern the family has named. Try to stimulate their curiosity and create an atmosphere that brings everyone's perspective into the game – "How does dad feel about the 'shouting mood?'" "How does your little sister feel about it?"

Check again: "Is this a pattern you recognise in your family?"

Step 3. Generalise (and consider change)
Determine if and how the interaction patterns discovered affected the difficulties that brought the family to therapy, and how the new understanding can be applied in their lives. Do they want to continue in these patterns? What alternative strategies could be developed, and what will they take with them? Make a plan for how the new strategies can be implemented in the family. If necessary, try them out while in the room to see how they feel.

Check again: "What do you think of this plan? Should it continue? Would you rather change the plan? Does the plan make sense to everybody? How does it feel now?"

Tips and tricks

It is not always necessary to be strict with each step, but less experienced professionals might be helped by going "by the book".

> ### Example
> During a family therapy session, two teenage children and their parents discover that the family's attempts to discuss and find solutions to the older boy's difficulties in school usually end with everyone else sitting in silence while the mother cries. When it happens at home, the father and children all leave the living room and go into their bedrooms or out into the garden. The family names this pattern "the silent moment" and can now begin to uncover what happens both between and inside them in that situation. They can also explore ideas on how they could handle things differently and stay in the room to test them.

Note: The exercise was developed in collaboration with psychotherapist and BA in philosophy, Mette Mørk.

MODEL **MBT-F LOOP**

Discovering and naming

Check

Check

Check

Generalise (and consider change)

Mentalize the moment

Contingent mirroring and deviant mirroring styles

During his first years, the child begins to learn that he can detect, categorise, articulate, and regulate his own emotions. This happens during typical evolutionary interactions where the child learns to master his emotions via the following process:

First, he recognises the adult's emotions as accurately as possible and then reflects those emotions in his own mind. Adults can use reflection to take the opportunity to turn the intensity of emotions either up or down. This means that the adult reflects the emotion in a slightly different manner from the way the baby perceives the emotion. Marked mirroring means that the child understands that the caregiver's mirroring teaches the child about his or her own emotional states. In the mother-child relationship, the mother controls the up and down volume. The child learns that emotions can be controlled through contact.

What to do?

The model can be used to understand how emotions are regulated during the development-promoting interaction. The model can also be used to analyse how the interaction between the child and caregiver takes place or has taken place. Finally, the model is used in psycho-education with parents, who, along with the therapist can analyse the interaction and develop ideas on how the interaction can promote more development.

Tips and tricks

It is easy for caregivers to engage in development-promoting interactions that include joy. One should also be curious about how anger, fear, and sadness manifest.

Example

A nine-year-old boy has a phobia about school. He is terrified when he goes to school in the morning. His mother is worried that he will not go. Every morning ends up in a vicious circle where the boy does not go to school. The mother comes to understand that the important thing is that she finds peace, and reflects that, above the anxiety she recognises in her son. By being calm and reflecting, she can help her son to control his anxiety by showing him (marked mirroring) that anxiety can be regulated.

MODEL DEVELOPMENT PROMOTING MIRRORING

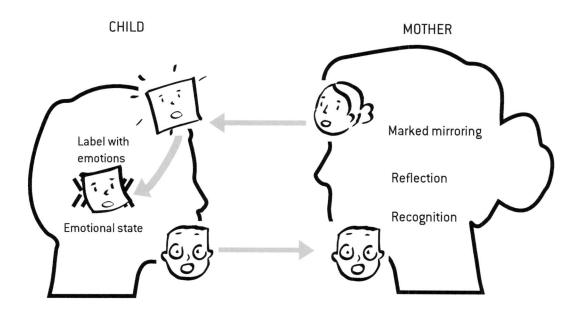

The mother recognises the child's emotional state as anxiety. She reflects on it and sends it back in the marked mirroring mode. That is, she sends back the same emotions, but with a different intensity. Through this change in intensity, the mother transmits to the child that we are now talking about what you are feeling (anxiety). When fear is displayed, the mother uses marked mirroring to lower the sense of intensity of the fear and anxiety (if the child was perhaps displaying a slight curiosity, the mother could increase the intensity of the mirroring to bring up the curiosity level). Through the marked mirroring, the child regulates his anxiety and learns to recognise the emotion. The child now has a label to use and identify "anxiety".

This interaction is the basis on which the child learns to detect, categorise, articulate, and regulate anxiety onwards.

MODEL DEVIANT MIRRORING STYLES

Overly involved communication

CHILD   MOTHER

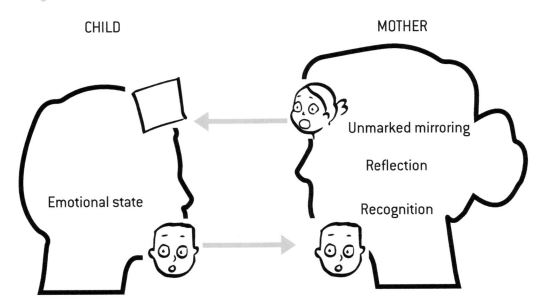

The child is anxious. The mother is as frightened as the child, and fails to reflect the anxiety so she mirrors the emotion back to the child in an unmarked manner. Therefore, the child doesn't recognise anxiety as his own emotion, he only sees that the mother is afraid. The child does not learn how to recognise or label his own anxiety. Instead, the child is left with an even greater sense of anxiety because he can see that the mother is afraid.

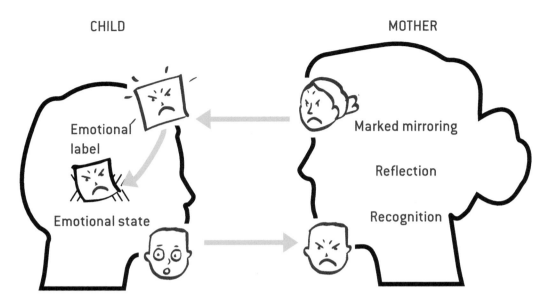

The child is anxious. The mother does not recognise it as anxiety, but instead sees it as "anger". "He's at it again." The mother engages in a marked mirroring of "anger".

When the mother mirrors the emotion in a marked way, the child comes to understand his anxiety as anger. The child thus develops an incorrect labelling of anxiety as anger, which confuses and divides the child's self-image.

The integrative model – the building blocks of mentalization in teaching and in therapy

This model integrates the core concepts of mentalization-based treatment for neglected and traumatised children and adolescents. The Open (ÅBENT) mind model is the basis for treatment. The treatment consists of the STORM model on the one hand and the intervention spectrum on the other. Together they form the framework for therapy.

Both the STORM model and intervention spectrum are models that can be used to monitor a client's sense of security and emotional intensity. If safety isn't secured, this is the main focus and if the emotions are running high, empathy and support should be the starting point. This is evident in the model, by the fact that mentalization-based treatment begins from the bottom.

The centre of the model is "the eye of the storm", which consists of a number of building blocks. These are the skills to be developed throughout the treatment.

What to do?

The model integrates all the central treatment models and can be used to create an overview of the combined theories and a course of treatment.

Tips and tricks

Use the model both in residential homes, therapy, and family therapy.

Example

A mother seeks anonymous advice. She says that she has come because her husband is forcing her to get help in understanding her relationship with her younger daughter, who has just turned one year old. The mother says that she actually does not care for her younger daughter, because she thinks she prevents her from being a good enough mother to her elder daughter, a three year old. As the conversation progresses, the mother says that the elder daughter suffered permanent injuries after the mother had an automobile accident when the older daughter was just a year old.

The mother says she never wanted more children. She wants to devote her life to her older daughter and her rehabilitation. The psychologist has a great desire to help the mother with integrating her trauma in relation to the traffic accident and process the losses suffered by her older daughter and then work to accept her daughter as she is today. She also knows she will have to work at building up the relationship with the younger daughter, whom the mother is not ready to have a mentalizing relationship to just yet. The therapist considers all the models in the guide and decides to use the "Building blocks for mentalization" when working with the mother. She realises she must start by using the (Open) ÅBENT mind to establish a sense of security while being supportive and empathetic at the same time. She must work her way slowly through the model.

MODEL BUILDING BLOCKS FOR MENTALIZATION-BASED TEACHING

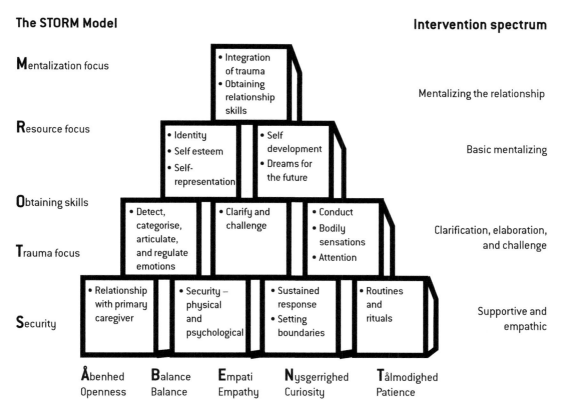

The STORM Model

Mentalization focus

Resource focus

Obtaining skills

Trauma focus

Security

- Integration of trauma
- Obtaining relationship skills

- Identity
- Self esteem
- Self-representation

- Self development
- Dreams for the future

- Detect, categorise, articulate, and regulate emotions

- Clarify and challenge

- Conduct
- Bodily sensations
- Attention

- Relationship with primary caregiver

- Security – physical and psychological

- Sustained response
- Setting boundaries

- Routines and rituals

Åbenhed — Openness
Balance — Balance
Empati — Empathy
Nysgerrighed — Curiosity
Tålmodighed — Patience

Intervention spectrum

Mentalizing the relationship

Basic mentalizing

Clarification, elaboration, and challenge

Supportive and empathic

Note: The model is developed in collaboration with research student Line Sangild Thimmer – an employee of Center for mentalisering.

Neglect

The following model contains examples of how four different types of neglect of care affect a child's difficulties with mentalization. The model can be applied to assess what kind of intervention is required in order to meet the child's needs.

What should you do?

Use the model to analyse what types of neglect the child has been exposed to by asking yourself:

- Has the child been exposed to physical damage from adults such as beating or other kinds of violence? Or sexual assault? **Active physical neglect.**

- Has the child been threatened? Does the child feel spoken to in a negative and humiliating way or has he been locked in a fixed negative role? **Active mental neglect.**

- Has the child been exposed to serious neglect/mistreatment from caregivers? For example, not having warm, clean clothes, not getting enough to eat or drink, living in messy or dirty conditions and receiving inadequate help with hygiene, having rotten teeth, or having a dirty nappy? **Passive physical neglect.**

- Has the child been mentally or emotionally neglected? Or has he not been offered the types of interactions needed for promoting development? **Passive mental neglect.**

Tips and tricks

It is important to realise what types of neglect have been suffered. It is important to the child's reactions and development as well as treatment planning (Christoffersen & DePanfilis, 2009).

Example

A twelve-year-old girl is brought to an institution. The staff notice that she adapts like a chameleon, depending on who she might be with at the moment. When she is not under supervision and under the radar, she has wild emotional swings. She has great difficulty in maintaining relationships with her peers. The staff feel that it is difficult to understand and know how to help a girl who cannot describe her history or inner life. Examination reveals that the girl has been living with her autistic father. Analysis of the neglect the girl has been exposed to makes it apparent that it is a case of passive mental neglect. Her father has not beaten or spoken rudely to her and she has been carefully cared for, but the father did not have any real contact or any way to mentalize with the girl. He has not been able to offer her any development-promoting interactions. By doing everything she could to fit in, the girl has managed to establish development promoting care from the people she has met.

OVERVIEW **NEGLECT**

	Physical	Mental
Active	Violence, sexual assault	Humiliating conversation, fixated negative role
Passive	Lack of food / drink, lack of help with basic hygiene such as clean nappy, clean clothes, etc.	Understimulation, absence of development-promoting relationships

Symptoms of violence – active physical neglect

The symptoms of violence are a person's unique way of learning to live with violence. One can not conclude directly from the symptoms that the child has been abused. The same symptoms can have different causes, but the following symptoms are characteristic of children living in families where violence is prevalent, so there is reason to be concerned about the child's well-being.

The symptoms can be viewed as a language explaining what has happened. For example, when a child is exposed to violence, gaps can appear in the small blood vessels near the skin's surface. This is a residual effect after the violence, but also a symptom that can be tracked down.

What to do?
The list can be used to reveal children who live with violence, and to understand the child's or adolescent's actions as reasonable and common, as you would expect when you have lived with violence.

Tips and tricks
The list of symptoms can also be used in working with violent parents in order to articulate the impact that their violence has on children. It can also be used with abused children to help them understand that their reactions are reasonable ways to deal with what they have lived with.

Example
A networking event is set up for a nine-year-old girl. Teachers are worried because the girl becomes violent when involved in conflicts with other children. She rarely participates in physical education class and seems scared if a teacher scolds her. She is very discouraged at school and lacks faith in herself. The school psychologist asks gently if there is any suspicion of domestic violence, and it becomes clear that the girl has often hinted that her mother beats her.

MODEL SYMPTOMS OF VIOLENCE –
ACTIVE PHYSICAL NEGLECT

- Visible marks (bruises, red marks indicating hitting, choking, or burning)

- Aggression

- Violent behaviour

- Difficulties in handling conflicts

- Signs of trauma

- Direct signs of failure to thrive at home

- Self-harm

- Somatic reactions

- Secretive and/or shameful behaviour

- Lack of trust/avoids specific people

- Anxiety

- Depression/worry

- No hope for the future

- Escapes into homework, school, fantasy worlds, or friends

- Frequent emergency room visits

- Avoids physical education class

- Difficulties with concentration/attention

- General failure to thrive

Source: Hagelquist and Skov, 2014.

Symptoms of sexual abuse – active physical neglect

The symptoms of sexual abuse are a person's unique way of mastering living with sexual assault. One can not conclude directly from the symptoms that sexual assault has occurred. The same symptoms can have different causes, but the following symptoms characterise children who have experienced sexual abuse, so there is reason to be concerned about the child's well-being.

One can see the symptoms as a language explaining what has happened. When a child is exposed to sexual abuse, she (or he) may receive positive attention if she behaves in a sexual manner. The child may therefore behave in a sexual manner with teachers and classmates. This can be a sign of living with sexual assault, but also a symptom that others can track.

What to do?

The list can be used to identify children who live with sexual assault, and to understand the child's reactions as a reasonable and normal reaction to living with sexual assault.

Tips and tricks

The symptoms list can be used with children who have been victims of sexual assault, to help them understand that their reactions are normal ways of coping with what they have experienced. It can also be used to help the child's network to understand her reactions.

Example
A girl who has been sexually abused will not take a shower and has very poor personal hygiene. Reviewing the list of symptoms helped her foster parents understand that this is a coping strategy from when she lived with abuse. They should therefore be careful and sensitive in their approach to teaching her about hygiene.

MODEL SYMPTOMS OF SEXUAL ABUSE –
ACTIVE PHYSICAL NEGLECT

- Overtly sexualised behaviour

- Excessive or age-inappropriate sexual play

- Excessive or age-inappropriate sexual talk

- Unusual or age-inappropriate knowledge of sexual themes

- Inappropriate touching

- Overtly sexualised in dress or body language

- Children younger than eleven years old can display anxiety about sex and sexually related topics

- Following their sexual debut, the child quickly engages in advanced sexual activity

- Physical symptoms and reactions

- Poor personal hygiene

- Mistrust – avoiding specific people

- Apathy – resignation and a sense of meaninglessness

- Depression/worry

- Silence

- No hope for the future

- Secretive, shameful

- Suicide attempts

- Escape into homework, school, fantasy world, or friends

- Self-abuse

- Anxiety

- Failure to thrive

- General dissatisfaction

Source: Cohen, Deblinger, Maedel, & Stauffer, 1999; Hagelquist, 2006.

Symptoms of psychological abuse – active mental neglect

The symptoms of psychological abuse are a person's unique way of mastering living with the abuse. One can not conclude directly from the symptoms that psychological abuse has occurred. The same symptoms can have different causes, but the following symptoms characterise children who have experienced psychological abuse, so there is reason to be concerned about the child's well-being.

One can see the symptoms as a language explaining what has happened. When a child is exposed to psychological abuse, he may be very insecure of himself. This can both be a sign of living with psychological abuse, and a symptom that can be tracked.

In adulthood, psychological abuse as a child has an impact on: social relationships, establishing relationships, and the ability to complete an education or hold a job.

What to do?

The list can be used to reveal children who live with psychological abuse, and to understand the child's or adolescent's actions as reasonable and common when you have lived with abuse.

Tips and tricks

The symptoms list can be used with children who have been victims of psychological abuse to help them understand that their reactions are normal ways of coping with what they have experienced.

Example

A boy who has been subjected to psychological abuse is scheduled to go on a skiing trip with his residential institution. The boy is convinced that he cannot learn to ski. He drones on continuously in the days leading up to the trip: "I can't do it. I'll ruin everything. It's so embarrassing that I have no control over my body." The boy's teachers are aware that he is reflecting what he has been told about his own incompetence. They are careful and gentle in cautiously challenging the boy, so that he not only becomes a fine skier, but he is also overly proud afterwards.

MODEL SYMPTOMS OF PSYCHOLOGICAL ABUSE – ACTIVE MENTAL NEGLECT

- Low self-esteem and a negative identity

- A basic sense of shame, helplessness, and unworthiness

- Learned helplessness

- Behavioural problems

- Social problems

- Difficulty concentrating

- Shame

- Anxiety

- Mistrust

Symptoms of neglect – passive physical neglect

The symptoms of passive physical neglect are a person's unique way of mastering living with neglect. One can not conclude directly from the symptoms that neglect has occurred. The same symptoms can have different causes, but the following symptoms characterise children who have experienced passive physical neglect, so there is reason to be concerned about the child's well-being.

One can view the symptoms as a language explaining what has happened. When a child is dropped off at daycare on Monday with a completely red and sore bottom, it may be a sign that the child has been in the same nappy all weekend. This can both be a sign of living with passive physical neglect, and a symptom that can be tracked.

What to do?

The list can be used to reveal children who live with passive physical neglect and to understand that the child or adolescent is reacting reasonably for one who has lived with neglect.

Tips and tricks

The symptoms list can be used with children who have been victims of passive physical neglect, to help them understand that their reactions are normal ways of coping with what they have experienced.

Example

An eleven-year-old boy who has been exposed to neglect eats and eats. It appears that he has not learned to control his hunger. His foster parents are concerned. He seems unable to stop and simply continues eating. Likewise, the boy cannot determine on his own whether he is warm or cold. Shortly after he moved in, the boy's foster mother suggested that he should wash and he got into the shower fully clothed. It was clear he had never taken a shower before.

MODEL SYMPTOMS OF NEGLECT –
PASSIVE PHYSICAL NEGLECT

- Cannot detect hunger or thirst

- Cannot sense personal physical boundaries

- Cannot determine cold/hot

- Lack of sensory stimulation

- Basic hygiene issues

- Hiding food

Symptoms of a lack of development enhancing interactions – passive mental neglect

A child's development depends on his being in a relationship in which the caregiver teaches him to register, categorise, articulate, and then control his mental states. In such a development-friendly environment, the child's innate potential is realised, and he develops a consistent and positive sense of self.

The symptoms of a lack of a development enhancing relationship are a person's unique way of mastering living with the neglect. The same symptoms can have different causes; for example, they may result from congenital problems, but the following symptoms also characterise children who have experienced a lack of development enhancing interactions, so there is reason to be concerned about the child's well-being.

One can view the symptoms as a language explaining what has happened. When the child has not been taught to pay attention, he can develop great problems with doing so. He may also have difficulties in regulating the abilities that normally develop in developmental enhancement interactions. These are the same skills/domains mentioned in the STORM model. This can both be a sign of a lack of development enhancing interactions, and a symptom that can be tracked.

What to do?
The list can be used to reveal children who live with a lack of development enhancing interaction and to understand that the child or adolescent is reacting reasonably for one who has lived with a lack of development enhancing interactions. It can also be used to see where to meet the child chronologically in order to offer the correct development enhancing interactions.

Tips and tricks
The symptoms list can be used to help the child's network in understanding his reactions.

Example
An eleven-year-old adopted girl suffered lack of development enhancing interactions for the first six years of her life when she lived in an orphanage in Africa. She has difficulty controlling virtually all of the six domains. Understanding this helps her foster parents realise that to offer her development enhancing interactions, they must handle her as a much younger child than her biological age indicates. They become aware that handling her as an ordinary eleven year old would be equivalent to asking a child in the first year of school to master the year nine curriculum.

MODEL SYMPTOMS OF LACK OF DEVELOPMENT ENHANCING INTERACTIONS – PASSIVE MENTAL NEGLECT

Emotions

Unable to recognise, categorise, articulate, and regulate emotions or recognise emotions in others.

Behaviour

Inability to meet standard age-appropriate expectations for behaviour such as eating well, going shopping, etc. Destructive, self-destructive behaviour. Reliving previous trauma. Poor survival and coping strategies.

Attention/cognition

Lacking the age-appropriate skills needed to sustain attention and focus in different contexts.

Lack of age-appropriate cognitive functioning. Failure to keep up in school and a lack of general knowledge: who is the president of the USA, etc.

Physical

Lacks the age-appropriate skills to regulate physical conditions such as cold and heat, to feel hunger and satiety, feel fatigue or feel relaxed, or feel and use age-appropriate motor skills.

Self

Lacks an experience of a total "Me" (self-representation) – with positive self-esteem as a result of having been mirrored positively. A lack of experiencing a positive and autonomous sense of "I" (self as an agent): the belief that one can exist positively in the world and succeed in achieving objectives and that actions and behaviour are recognised and result in the desired outcomes.

Relationships

A lack of age-appropriate skills in relationships: missing ability to have close and positive relationships with others, including teachers, pets, neighbours, family members, or others.

Part 2

Psycho-education is used to support the neglected and traumatised to find a better understanding of themselves and what it is they are struggling with. The models in this part of the guide can provide a language for understanding and handling the child's inner condition and relationships with others.

The models concerning trauma and trauma reactions are particularly important because many vulnerable children have no knowledge of trauma or post-traumatic reactions. Psycho-education offers them insight to normal reactions to the traumatic events they have experienced and assures them that they are not going crazy or are particularly vulnerable and fragile.

WHAT TO DO?
Use the models in Part 2 directly with the child, with families, with their network, or within organisations. You do not have to know the child's unique history or trauma history in detail to use the models – it can be a good idea to describe the models as a general way that someone might feel and let the models be the foundation for mentalizing conversations.

TIPS AND TRICKS
There are strong forces at work within trauma; when working with them, it is important to use your ability to mentalize. In a traumatic situation, the child's boundaries have most likely been been violated. This can attach shame to the trauma. Therefore, it is important not to recreate situations where the child feels that his boundaries are being crossed or he feels ashamed. Trauma also creates a sense of loneliness and a feeling in the child that he has done something wrong. By talking about and normalising traumatic reactions, it is possible to work to lessen those feelings.

EXAMPLE
A group of vulnerable pregnant women take a course using the models from this part of the guide. It turns out that each of the women has problems mentalizing and has had traumatic experiences. The women are very engaged by the models because they are motivated to give their children a better start in life than they have had.

Mentalization and psycho-education

Psycho-education is an important part of mentalization-based treatment. Children, parents, foster parents, and educators should be instructed in mentalizing. To become better at mentalizing, it is important to understand what mentalization is and that one is aware that one has to work on developing mentalization abilities.

Mentalization means to have "focus on mental states in oneself or in others, especially in connection with the explanation of behaviour" (Bateman & Fonagy, 2007, p. 33). The mental conditions that affect behaviour can include: emotions/feelings, thoughts, needs, goals, and reasons (Allen, Fonagy, & Bateman, 2010).

What to do?

In every context where mentalization is part of the work, there must be clarity on what mentalizing is. One can talk about the concept. Be explicit about and enhance mentalizing interaction and hand out the model of mentalization.

Tips and tricks

One can see mentalizing as a muscle to be trained. At its toughest, mentalizing can be like that last, almost impossible, lift at the gym. This is when it gives the most benefit. Try to turn on the lights in every part of the brain involved in mentalizing when it feels like it is most difficult. For example, be sympathetic to your boyfriend while he behaves stupidly. Look behind the behaviour of your foster child who is throwing a tantrum. See yourself from the outside, while you are scolding someone within the context of your job. Try to understand the mother who shouts that she will make sure that her daughter will be removed from her foster family because she has become too close to them.

> **Example**
> A mother says: "It suddenly makes sense. What I need to do is understand what I am feeling and what my daughter feels when we quarrel. Only then should I say something."

MODEL WHAT DOES MENTALIZATION MEAN, AND WHY IS IT IMPORTANT?

Mentalization is about:

- Being able to understand the mental states behind your own and another's behaviour
- Better understanding yourself and others
- Seeing yourself from the outside and others from the inside
- Understanding misunderstandings.
- Looking behind behaviours.

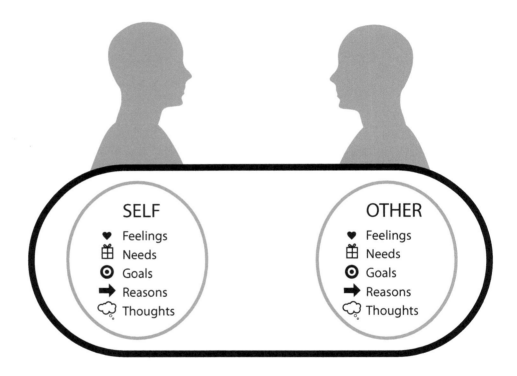

WHY MENTALIZATION IS IMPORTANT

It makes it easier to understand oneself

A thirty-two-year-old woman has a birthday. Her boyfriend looks expectantly at her while she opens her gift. But she feels like crying and cursing and says a sour "Thank you." The gift is exactly what she wanted, so she is confused by her own behaviour until she remembers that when she was little, her mother was not good at finding gifts but still sat and stared expectantly when she opened them up. Her mother was greatly disappointed when she showed no enthusiasm. Once she understands her own behaviour, she hurries to give her boyfriend a kiss and a hug.

It makes it easier to understand others

An eleven month old throws his dummy out of his pram again and again. His mother retrieves it every time, but is feeling angrier and angrier until she pauses and remembers that her child is learning how gravity works.

When one understands others, it is easier to control and handle strong emotions

A mother heads home from work. She is tired and knows that when she gets home, she has to prepare for guests due that evening. She is therefore thankful that her mother has been over earlier to clean. But when she comes home, she sees that someone has been cooking in the kitchen, dirtying cake bowls and scattering batter and crumbs everywhere. She is upset and angry. When her daughters appear in the doorway and say that they have baked her favourite cake, she turns down her emotions and thanks her daughters and asks them to help clean up.

The emotional compass as psycho-education

The Fonagy group (Allen, Fonagy, & Bateman, 2010) considers emotions the most important path to mentalization and say that the importance of our emotions can not be overstated. Emotions are the inner compass that helps us feel what is right and wrong.

What to do?

When the emotional compass is introduced, it is important to convey that basic emotions are found in all cultures (Berk, 1994). When a child in Africa expresses anxiety, a mother from China recognises that emotion as anxiety. Emotions help everyone find out which way to go and what feels right and wrong. The benefits of registering, categorising, and verbalising all the different basic emotions of the compass – especially the negative ones – can be taught.

Tips and tricks

It may be a good idea to use general examples to describe the importance of also being able to use the emotions that one might perceive as negative. For example, it has been important for human survival for the species to be able to feel fear. Without that emotion, we would not have survived encounters with wild animals. One can also find examples that correspond to problems that a child recognises. When one feels disgust, it can be an important signal that something is not good for one or one's body. It may also be important for someone to sometimes get angry and stay angry. Otherwise, there is a risk that others will cross your limits so often that you forget where your own boundaries are.

Example

A sixteen-year-old girl is going to a psychologist. She says that she is now in high school and can no longer handle the pressure. One day, she began to cry as she was leaving school and she has been in bed since. She has lived alone with her mother, who is an alcoholic. She has always been the adult in the home, and there has never been room for her emotions. If she showed any emotion other than joy, her mother would respond by crying and drinking.

During therapy, the psychologist moves through the emotional compass. He says that we need all our emotions – that they are equal on the compass. The girl says she always believed that the world would fall apart if she was angry; that if she started to cry she would never stop, and her fear has now become reality. The psychologist explains that it is indeed fortunate that this is happening now, so she can learn that her sadness is an important signal that there is too much work and too little fun in her life. "You can use the anger to learn that you have to take care of yourself and not just continue to work mindlessly."

MODEL THE EMOTIONAL COMPASS FOR CHILDREN

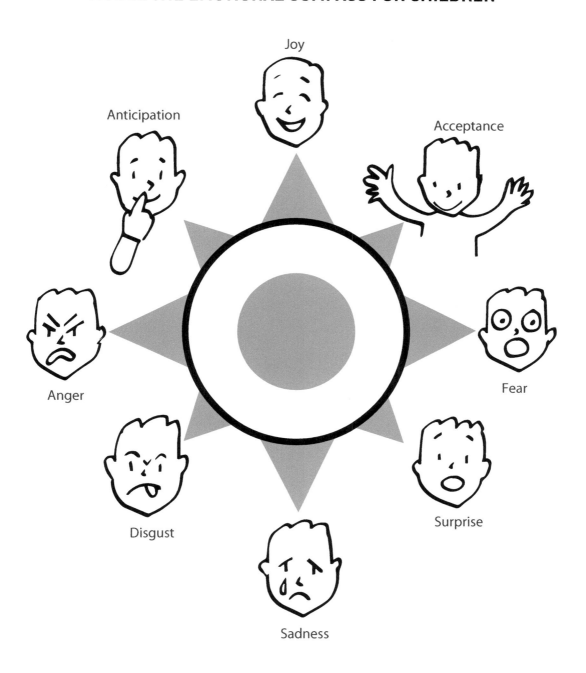

Diagnostic criteria for PTSD

The diagnosis for post-traumatic stress disorder (PTSD) is described in the American diagnosis system DSM-V, the *Diagnostic and Statistical Manual of Mental Disorders*. This diagnosis is used in all mentalization literature.

For PTSD to be considered, the person must have been directly or indirectly exposed to a tremendously stressful event, such as experiencing or witnessing violence, rape, robbery, war, or a serious accident. Teaching traumatised people about the effects of trauma is the most important element of trauma treatment. When mentalizing with a traumatised child, it is important to know about PTSD to understand the mental states of trauma.

What to do?

PTSD symptoms are recognised as normal human reactions to extreme circumstances. It is also important for the traumatised person to know that the condition can change, and that he can be normal again. By hearing about the effects of trauma, the traumatised child realises that he is not alone, and that he is not crazy or strange and that post-traumatic reactions are normal.

Tips and tricks

Maintain your professionalism and be aware that the person you are working with in either education or therapy may have been traumatised. People do not spontaneously talk about post-traumatic reactions.

Example

A sixteen-year-old girl talks about her childhood of abuse and violence. She has been given a diagnosis of PTSD and is completely overwhelmed with its accuracy. "That is exactly how I feel," she repeats again and again. She carries the diagnosis with her. Following a move to another part of the country, her treatment is suspended. Two years later, she begins working with a psychologist. The first thing she does is take the diagnosis from her handbag. She says: "I have had many handbags since I got this, but I always move this over to the new one. It helps me when I do not understand my own actions. I also show it to the teachers I like best, so they can better understand me."

MODEL PTSD ACCORDING TO THE DSM-V

(DSM-V, pp. 271–174)
Diagnostic Criteria

Posttraumatic Stress Disorder

Note: The following criteria apply to adults, adolescents, and children older than 6 years. For children 6 years and younger, see corresponding criteria below.

A. Exposure to actual or threatened death, serious injury, or sexual violence in one (or more) of the following ways:

1. Directly experiencing the traumatic event(s).
2. Witnessing, in person, the event(s) as it occurred to others.
3. Learning that the traumatic event(s) occurred to a close family member or close friend. In cases of actual or threatened death of a family member or friend, the event(s) must have been violent or accidental.
4. Experiencing repeated or extreme exposure to the aversive details of the traumatic event(s) (e.g., first responders collecting human remains; police officers repeatedly exposed to details of child abuse).
   Note: Criterion A4 does not apply to exposure through electronic media, television, movies or pictures, unless this exposure is work related.

B. Presence of one (or more) of the following intrusion symptoms associated with the traumatic event(s), beginning after the traumatic event(s) occurred:

1. Recurrent, involuntary, and intrusive distressing memories of the traumatic event(s).
   Note: In children older than 6 years, repetitive play may occur in which themes or aspects of the traumatic event(s) are expressed.
2. Recurrent distressing dreams in which the content and/or affect of the dream are related to the traumatic event(s).
   Note: In children, there may be frightening dreams without recognizable content.
3. Dissociative reactions (e.g., flashbacks) in which the individual feels or acts as if the traumatic event(s) were recurring. (Such reactions may occur on a continuum, with the most extreme expression being a complete loss of awareness of present surroundings.
   Note: In children, trauma-specific reenactment may occur in play.

4. Intense or prolonged psychological distress at exposure to internal or external cues that symbolize or resemble an aspect of the traumatic event(s).
5. Marked physiological reactions to internal or external cues that symbolize or resemble an aspect of the traumatic event(s).

C. Persistent avoidance of stimuli associated with the traumatic event(s), beginning after the traumatic event(s) occurred, as evidenced by one or both of the following:

1. Avoidance of or efforts to avoid distressing memories, thoughts, or feelings about or closely associated with the traumatic event(s).
2. Avoidance of or efforts to avoid external reminders (people, places, conversations, activities, things, situations) that arouse distressing memories, thoughts, or feelings about or closely associated with the traumatic event(s).

D. Negative alterations in cognitions and mood associated with the traumatic event(s), beginning or worsening after the traumatic event(s) occurred, as evidenced by two (or more) of the following:

1. Inability to remember an important aspect of the traumatic event(s) (typically due to dissociative amnesia and not to other factors such as head trauma, alcohol, or drugs).
2. Persistent and exaggerated negative beliefs or expectations about oneself, others, or the world (e.g., "I am bad", "No one can be trusted", "The world is completely dangerous", "My whole nervous system is permanently ruined.").
3. Persistent, distorted cognitions about the cause or consequences of the traumatic event(s) that lead the individual to blame himself/herself or others.
4. Persistent negative emotional state (e.g., fear, horror, anger, guilt, or shame).
5. Markedly diminished interest or participation in significant activities.
6. Feelings of detachment or estrangement from others.
7. Persistent inability to experience positive emotions (e.g., inability to experience happiness, satisfaction, or loving feelings).

E. Marked alterations in arousal and reactivity associated with the traumatic event(s), beginning or worsening after the traumatic event(s) occurred, as evidenced by two (or more) of the following:

1. Irritable behavior and anger outburst (with little or no provocation) typically expressed as verbal or physical aggression toward people or objects.
2. Reckless or self-destructive behavior.
3. Hypervigilance.

4. Exaggerated startle response.
5. Problems with concentration.
6. Sleep disturbance (e.g., difficulty falling asleep or staying asleep or restless sleep).

F. Duration of the disturbance (Criteria B, C, D and E) is more than 1 month.
G. The disturbance causes clinically significant distress or impairment in social, occupational, or other important areas of functioning.
H. The disturbance is not attributable to the physiological effects of a substance (e.g., medication, alcohol) or another medical condition.

Specify whether:

With dissociative symptoms: The individual's symptoms meet the criteria for posttraumatic stress disorder, and in addition, in response to the stressor, the individual experiences persistent or recurrent symptoms of either of the following:

1. **Depersonalization**: Persistent or recurrent experiences of feeling detached from, and as if one were an outside observer of, one's mental processes or body (e.g., feeling as though one were in a dream; feeling a sense of unreality of self or body or of time moving slowly).
2. **Derealization**: Persistent or recurrent experiences of unreality of surroundings (e.g., the world around the individual is experienced as unreal, dreamlike, distant, or distorted).
   Note: To use this subtype, the dissociative symptoms must not be attributable to the physiological effects of a substance (e.g., blackouts, behavior during alcohol intoxication) or another medical condition (e.g., complex partial seizures).

Specify if:

With delayed expression: If the full diagnostic are not met until at least six months after the event (although the onset and expression of some symptoms can be immediate).

Posttraumatic stress disorder for children 6 years and younger

A. In children 6 years and younger, exposure to actual or threatened death, serious injury, or sexual violence in one (or more) of the following ways:

1. Directly experiencing the traumatic event(s).
2. Witnessing, in person, the event(s) as it occurred to others, especially primary caregivers.
   Note: Witnessing does not include events that are witnessed only in electronic media, television, movies, or pictures.

3. Learning that the traumatic event(s) occurred to a parent or caregiving figure.

B. Presence of one (or more) of the following intrusion symptoms associated with the traumatic event(s), beginning after the traumatic event(s) occurred:

1. Recurrent, involuntary, and intrusive distressing memories of the traumatic event(s).
   Note: Spontaneous and intrusive memories may not necessarily appear distressing and may be expressed as play reenactment.
2. Recurrent distressing dreams in which the content and/or affect of the dream are related to the traumatic event(s).
   Note: It may not be possible to ascertain that the frightening content is related to the traumatic event.
3. Dissociative reactions (e.g., flashbacks) in which the child feels or acts as if the traumatic event(s) were recurring. (Such reactions may occur on a continuum, with the most extreme expression being a complete loss of awareness of present surroundings). Such trauma-specific reenactment may occur in play.
4. Intense or prolonged psychological distress at exposure to internal or external cues that symbolize or resemble an aspect of the traumatic event(s).
5. Marked physiological reactions reminders of the traumatic event(s).

C. One (or more) of the following symptoms, representing either persistent avoidance of stimuli associated with the traumatic event(s), or negative alterations in cognitions and mood associated with the traumatic event(s), must be present, beginning after the event(s) or worsening after the event(s):

Persistent avoidance of stimuli
1. Avoidance of or efforts to avoid activities, places, or physical reminders that arouse recollections of the traumatic event(s).
2. Avoidance of or efforts to avoid people, conversations, or interpersonal situations that arouse recollections of the traumatic event(s).

Negative alterations in cognitions
3. Substantially increased frequency of negative emotional states (e.g., fear, guilt, sadness, shame, confusion).
4. Markedly diminished interest or participation in significant activities, including constriction of play.
5. Socially withdrawn behavior.
6. Persistent reduction in expression of positive emotions.

D. Alterations in arousal and reactivity associated with the traumatic event(s), beginning or worsening after the traumatic event(s) occurred, as evidenced by two (or more) of the following:

1. Irritable behavior and angry outbursts (with little or no provocation) typically expressed as verbal or physical aggression toward people or objects (including extreme temper tantrums).
2. Hypervigilance.
3. Exaggerated startle response.
4. Problems with concentration.
5. Sleep disturbance (e.g., difficulty falling or staying asleep or restless sleep).

E. The duration of the disturbance is more than 1 month.
F. The disturbance causes clinically significant distress or impairment in relationships with parents, siblings, peers, or other caregivers or with school behavior.
G. The disturbance is not attributable to the physiological effects of a substance (e.g., medication or alcohol) or another medical condition.

Specify whether:
With dissociative symptoms: The individual's symptoms meet the criteria for posttraumatic stress disorder, and the individual experiences persistent or recurrent symptoms of either of the following:

1. **Depersonalization**: Persistent or recurrent experiences of feeling detached from, and as if one were an outside observer of, one's mental processes or body (e.g., feeling as though one were in a dream; feeling a sense of unreality of self or body or of time moving slowly).
2. **Derealisation**: Persistent or recurrent experiences of unreality of surroundings (e.g., the world around the individual is experienced as unreal, dreamlike, distant, or distorted).
   Note: To use this subtype, the dissociative symptoms must not be attributable to the physiological effects of a substance (e.g., blackouts) or another medical condition (e.g., complex partial seizures).

Specify if:
With delayed expression: If the full diagnostic criteria are not met until at least 6 months after the event (although the onset and expression of some symptoms may be immediate).

Source: American Psychiatric Association 2014.

PTSD in children

When the PTSD diagnosis was first developed in 1980, awareness that children could also suffer from trauma was just beginning. The prevailing belief at the time was that children were resilient to trauma, partially because they do not necessarily show signs of post-traumatic stress (Hagelquist, 2012). We now know that children can be traumatised, and we are constantly discovering new contexts in which it can happen – for example, in recent years we have become aware that children who witness domestic violence can develop PTSD (Kilpatrick & Williams, 1997).

Trauma has a decisive influence on what happens inside a child's mind as it colours the mind in a way that no other experience can. It can be difficult for children who have suffered neglect and trauma to verbalise their feelings and thoughts. They often think that they must be insane because they suffer post-traumatic stress reactions. If they do not get help to normalise their reactions, they will end up feeling lonely and like there is something wrong with them.

What to do?

Tell the child about post-traumatic stress reactions. Some children think and feel and do things they never thought or felt before the incident. Tell the child that it is normal to have such thoughts and feelings. In fact, it is the brain's way of trying to understand the traumatic incident the child has experienced, and that all brains respond exactly the same way. The models on the following pages show how the ostrich experiences different post-trauma stress reactions. If the child does not speak up spontaneously, one can ask whether he is familiar with feeling that way. A monologue about another child who has had a similar experience can also be effective.

Tips and tricks

Boys are often ashamed of having post-traumatic reactions. When working with them, it might be a good idea to talk about the symptoms as something often seen in soldiers. It may be the boy will find it more acceptable to have the same symptoms as someone who has been sent out to defend his country than it is to have flashbacks because he has seen his mother being abused.

Example

A teenage girl in an institution is shocked when she sees an educator shave. Even though they had previously had a very good relationship, she will no longer talk to him. It is only when she sees the drawing of the ostrich that "will not see anything resembling the incident" that she understands. She said that her father would always abuse her just after he had shaved and her mother had gone to work.

MODEL NORMAL REACTIONS AFTER HAVING EXPERIENCED SOMETHING VIOLENT

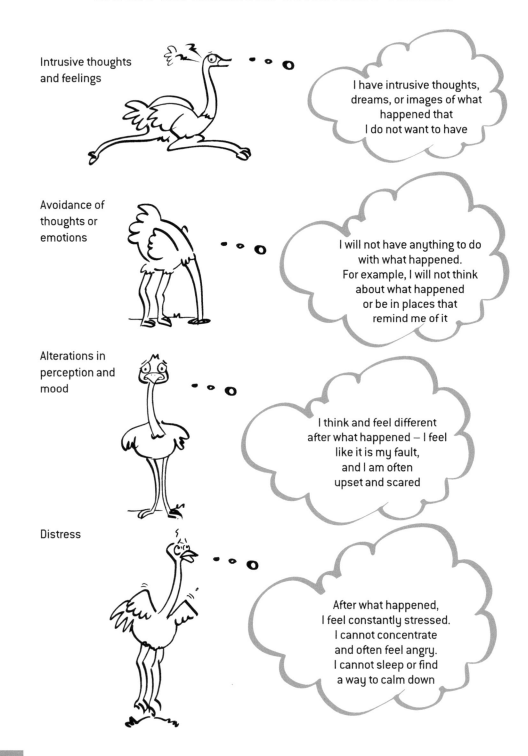

Intrusive thoughts and feelings

I have intrusive thoughts, dreams, or images of what happened that I do not want to have

Avoidance of thoughts or emotions

I will not have anything to do with what happened. For example, I will not think about what happened or be in places that remind me of it

Alterations in perception and mood

I think and feel different after what happened – I feel like it is my fault, and I am often upset and scared

Distress

After what happened, I feel constantly stressed. I cannot concentrate and often feel angry. I cannot sleep or find a way to calm down

Developmental trauma

In connection with the development of the latest edition of the US diagnostic system DSM-V, a number of American theorists tried to have a new diagnosis included. Their reasoning was that traditional trauma diagnoses like PTSD do not adequately take into account reactions following trauma that develop in children living with repetitive trauma from their primary caregivers. They failed to get the diagnosis included, but the concept lives on in research, theories, and the development of models of care for neglected and traumatised children and adolescents. The basic idea behind this trauma diagnosis/understanding is that as a result of their upbringing, neglected and traumatised children and adolescents are primarily concerned with survival rather than development, and thus will have difficulties in a number of areas such as the regulation of emotions, attention/cognition, behaviour, self-awareness, relationships, and physical well-being (van der Kolk, 2005a, 2005b).

What to do?

The developmental trauma disorder understanding is primarily useful for professionals and educators in their work with vulnerable teens/adults who are relatively adept in cognitive functioning. It describes all the complex facets and reactions experienced by those who have lived with neglect and trauma. Thus it offers a nuanced understanding of the behaviour of vulnerable children and adolescents. The developmental trauma understanding's starting point of explaining, why the symptoms arise, makes it possible for the mental states behind the behaviour of neglected and traumatised children to be accommodated within the understanding.

Tips and tricks

Start a collaborative meeting concerning a traumatised child with teaching about developmental trauma disorder, creating a common technical basis for understanding a child's behaviour, thereby paving the way for mentalization.

Example

We are at a collaborative meeting concerning a sixteen-year-old boy. He smokes marijuana every day and takes harder drugs at weekends. He was just handed a suspended sentence for armed robbery. He is a member of a local biker club and still looks for kicks stealing cars. He has an explosive temper and a confused sense of empathy – he seems to enjoy ridiculing the more vulnerable adolescents at the home. He is often ill. Whenever he is sick, he is convinced that it is life-threatening. As a result, he has logged a large number of casualty and doctor visits. Educators and teachers find it difficult to use mentalization with the boy, but developmental trauma disorder helps them recall his history of violence, failure, and loss, and that his behaviour is an expression of the coping strategies he developed as a child.

MODEL DEVELOPMENTAL TRAUMA DISORDER

A. Exposure
1. Multiple or chronic exposure to one or more forms of developmentally adverse interpersonal trauma (eg, abandonment, betrayal, physical assaults, sexual assaults, threats to bodily integrity, coercive, emotional abuse, witnessing violence and death).
2. Subjective experience (eg, rage, betrayal, fear, resignation, defeat, shame).

B. Triggered pattern of repeated dysregulation in response to trauma cues Dysregulation (high or low) in presence of cues. Changes persist and do not return to baseline; not reduced in intensity by consious awareness.
   - Affective.
   - Somatic (eg, physiological, motoric, medical).
   - Behavioral (eg, re-enactment, cutting).
   - Cognitive (eg, thinking that it is happening again, confusion, dissociation, depersonalization).
   - Relational (eg, clinging, oppositional, distrustful, compliant).
   - Self-attribution (eg, self-hate, blame).

C. Persistently Altered Attributions and Expectancies
   - Negative self-attribution.
   - Distrust of protective caregiver.
   - Loss of expectancy of protection by others.
   - Loss of trust in social agencies to protect.
   - Lack of recourse to social justice/retribution.
   - Inevitability of future victimization.

D. Functional Impairment
   - Educational.
   - Familial.
   - Peer.
   - Legal.
   - Vocational.

How you as a parent can help your traumatised child

Fonagy believes that parents are the best trauma therapists (Allen, Fonagy, & Bateman, 2010). If the child's parents are able to master the trauma in a constructive way or to take care of the child's needs, it will protect the child against developing trauma-reactions and serve as a protective factor against the child developing trauma symptoms (Cohen, Mannarino, & Deblinger, 2006; Friedman, Keane, & Resick, 2007). Trauma often causes parents to forget their strengths. It is important to support parents to be the best trauma therapists they can be. When children receive the proper support from their parents, they are actually more resilient than adults when it comes to trauma (Levine & Kline, 2007). This knowledge can be used to help children and adolescents who have been exposed to violent events.

What to do?

Since we know that children affected by trauma feel powerless, it is essential to return power to the parents. This means that parents need to be reminded that they can be something special in relation to their own child. Review the three points that parents need to be aware of to be good trauma therapists (see next page). Possibly mention Rudolph Giuliano, the mayor of New York City, who, following the 11 September, 2001 attack on the World Trade Centre, went around the streets and radiated a rock solid position while assuring the public that everything would be good again. He explained how he would deal with reconstruction – nothing turned out as he said, but it didn't matter: he radiated the confidence of an adult leader who was charting a direction while everything was in chaos. Americans loved him for it. Try to get the parents to be their child's Rudolph Giuliano.

Tips and tricks

It is important that the therapist is a role model and is able to function as a calming influence for the parents and show that the treatment is stable during difficult times, and that caregivers are supported in creating a comprehensive history of the traumatic situation. In the case of sexual assault, there can be special circumstances if the case has been referred to the police, but it is never forbidden for parents to comfort or listen to their child – lawsuit or not. Parents should avoid asking questions like, "Did he touch your vagina?" There are only two possible answers to that question, as opposed to the open question, "Where did he touch you?"

Example

A father and his ten-year-old son are involved in a serious car accident in which the oncoming motorist is killed. During the ensuing chaos, the father comforts his son by telling him that everything will be fine and that the ambulance is on its way. After they are checked out at the hospital, the father picks up sweets like they do every Friday. As time passes they discuss the incident often, always aware of the boy's needs at the moment. They also visit the dead man's grave.

MODEL HOW YOU AS A PARENT CAN HELP YOUR TRAUMATISED CHILD

Parents or other caregivers are the best trauma therapists. Parental support for a traumatised child will help him more easily cope with the trauma. The most important things to do are:

1. The adult should help affect regulate the child – comfort and contain the child's emotions and be a role model for how to deal with all the difficulties.
2. Daily life should be restored. Do everyday things: get up at the usual time, go to football practice, get homework done, and enjoy the usual weekend treats. Re-establishing the everyday rhythm helps normalise the situation.
3. Adults should support the child in creating a shared narrative of the traumatic situation – talk with the child about what happened. Show that you want to answer questions, and you will discuss the experience – even if it's hard. If possible, revisit the place where the trauma occurred and talk about it.

MacLean's triune brain theory

MacLean's triune brain theory is based on human evolution, and is a model for examining the brain's evolutionary development. The model is used in trauma literature to describe what happens when a human being is traumatised (MacLean, 1990).

The idea of the model is that the brain has a hierarchical structure in which the highest functions only work in conjunction with the lower functions, while lower functions can work independently of the higher functions. This means that when a person is traumatised, the most primitive parts of the brain take over and there is no access to the more rational parts of the brain.

The model can be used to explain that when a traumatised child is re-traumatised or overwhelmed by strong emotions, the parts of the brain which handle rational decisions, overview, and language are not working. This means that it is a waste of time to try to rationalise and explain things to an overly emotional child. The child needs to be reassured before it will be possible to communicate with the thinking brain. The brain in this model is divided into a reptile brain, a mammalian brain, and a thinking brain.

What to do?

Describe to the child's parents and their network how the brain is divided into three parts:

1. The reptilian brain
   The part of the brain we share with reptiles developed first evolutionarily and can cope with autonomous processes and where automatic survival behaviour such as fight, flight, or freeze are the only options.

2. The mammalian brain
   The part of the brain that we have in common with mammals. Emotions and attachment are located in this part of the brain.

3. The thinking brain
   The part of the brain that developed the most recently, evolutionarily speaking. The thinking human brain, which includes language, can process information cognitively and rationally and enables us to engage in long-term planning. Many important brain functions relating to mentalization are found in this part of the brain.

Tips and tricks

The model is an easy way to explain the complex processes that take place when humans are exposed to trauma. Remember that it is only a model, and there is a risk of oversimplifying complex brain functions and forgetting that the brain works as a cohesive, integrated unit.

Example

A six-year-old boy continually beats another boy with whom he has a conflict. The boy's teacher is shocked, believing that a child that can attack someone so severely must be a psychopath. Using the triune brain theory model, the boy's social worker explains that it is possible that he is so traumatised that he reacts primitively when he feels threatened. So he is like a crocodile biting and thinking only of survival and the fight. When the boy is calmer, attempts can be made to communicate with his thinking brain.

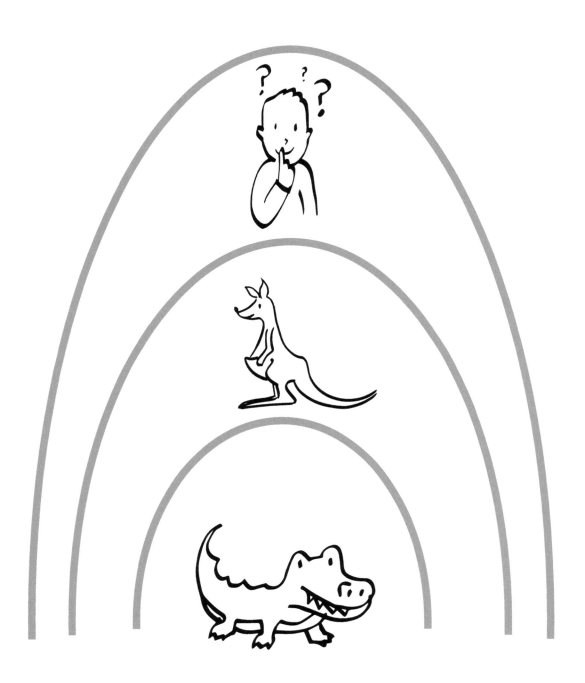

Fight, flight, freeze

When a person is terrified, his reactions are reduced to reflexes largely without conscious control. The typical reactions that occur when anxiety is highest are the reflexes that man shares with the most primitive species. The reactions are fight, flight, or freeze (scared stiff), and these can be constructive in a traumatic situation. They mean that people in dangerous situations only expend energy on strategies that ensure survival, and do not use the parts of the brain that can, for example, mentalize or perform more complex assessments.

Problems arise when these responses continue to be active once the danger is past. For the traumatised child, this means that when he experiences situations reminding him of the trauma, he reacts in the same way as he did when responding to the traumatic situation.

What to do?

Tell the child's network or parents how the brain reacts in connection with trauma.

Tips and tricks

Use humour. Tell them that if they encounter a man with a gun on a dark night, it would be a bad idea to begin to wonder what kind of gun it is or how much he paid for it.

Remember that many children may have fight-flight-freeze reactions which date back to prelinguistic trauma. One can easily understand the child's reactions using this terminology without knowing the origin of the original trauma.

Example

A seven-year-old boy has experienced repeated violence at the hands of his mother. Whenever his mother was angry, he protected himself by running to a neighbour's house. At a networking event, the boy's new teacher says that he tries to run away at the smallest reprimand. The boy's foster mother says the fight–flight–freeze reactions are signs that the boy is using escape strategies from the previous traumatic situation.

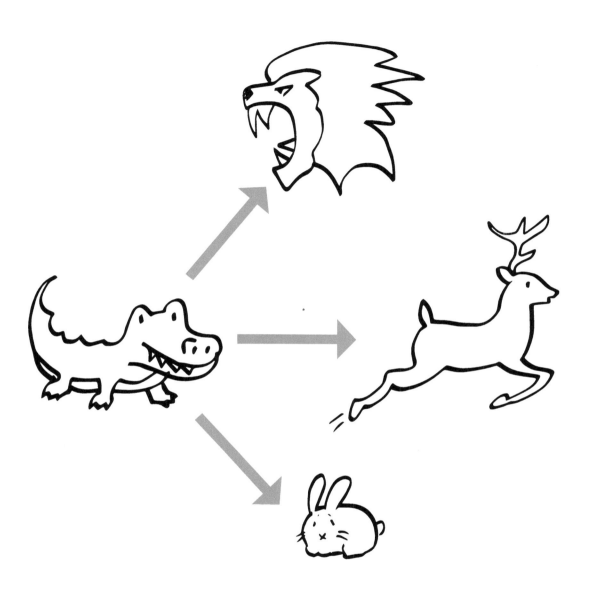

Protective factors in trauma

When a person is traumatised, there are a number of factors that protect against the following reactions (see model).

What to do?

The list can be used at collaborative meetings or just to support a trauma victim – regardless of the trauma, culture, or age – in explaining what has helped other trauma victims.

Tips and tricks

It may be important to know that methods for easing trauma are not advanced rocket science, but rather are common ways to show real concern for other people. In fact, we all know what we should do when others are having problems.

Think of what you would need and do not make it more complicated than it is.

Example

Five adults who have managed to break bad trauma patterns explain what made the difference for them. They all said, despite their very different traumas and life stories, that the factors listed in the model helped them in their respective ways to break free of trauma.

MODEL PROTECTIVE FACTORS IN TRAUMA

The factors that protect against post-traumatic reactions are:

- Social support
- Practical help and support
- Feeling understood
- Sharing traumatic experiences with others
- Understanding that post-traumatic processes and reactions are not "abnormal"
- Ability to share own coping strategies with others
- Belief in own coping skills
- Hope
- Optimism
- Positive expectations
- Belief that it is possible to influence own life and future
- Belief that others have the traumatised person's interests at heart
- Practical resources – jobs, money, home

Source: United States Department of Veterans Affairs

Lies

When people are lied to, it arouses strong emotions like anger, fear, shame, and sorrow. This often leads to an interruption in mentalization. This can be lengthy, and you may find that it is hard to be mentalizing with a person who has lied to you. Children who have been exposed to trauma and failures in care are more likely to lie than other children. At the same time, they have a greater need for mentalization than other children. This is an unfortunate mix. Understanding the types of lies and how to deal with them is important when working with children who lie (Feldman, 2009).

Lies tell us something about the mental state of the liar. Therefore lies should lead to curiosity about the mental state of the person telling the lie – especially the intention of the lie – and also the mental state of the person being lied to.

What to do?

On the following page is a model of the four different kinds of lies: white lies, cosmetic lies, deliberate lies, and cover stories.

Using the model, one can analyse what kind of lie you have been exposed to and get ideas about how to work with the lie.

Tips and tricks

Deliberate lies are the most rare. You may believe that the lie you are hearing is a deliberate lie, even though it may be another type. It is good to be vigilant if you find yourself thinking, for example, "She is lying on purpose and to do harm."

Example
A sixteen-year-old girl says that her best friend was murdered over the weekend. The girl said that she arrived at the scene before her friend died and sat with her until the police and ambulance arrived. Her foster parents are shocked and do everything to comfort her. When it turns out that the girl's friend is alive and well, her foster parents are frustrated, but they know that as a child, the girl lived with a mother who was a drug addict and that she often sat with her mother's head in her lap while her mother was wasted. The girl often worried that her mother had died, when she disappeared into her own universe. The foster parents suspect that the story is a cover story, and use this understanding to help the girl with her trauma history, without losing their ability to mentalize with her.

MODEL **VARIOUS KINDS OF LIES**

When confronting a lie, it is important to understand the mental state of the liar. One way to better understand is to find out what kind of lie is being told. The four forms of lying are:

White lies	Work
Basically social. They are told to live up to social norms, to avoid embarrassing situations, to support others, or to further a conversation.	Help the child to find other ways to say difficult things rather than through a lie. Traumatised children need more support in this area than other children.
Cosmetic lies	**Work**
The person lying feels inferior and is attempting to look or feel better.	Remember the correlation between low self-esteem and cosmetic lies. Children who tells cosmetic lies are vulnerable to criticism and punishment. The person who suffers the most from cosmetic lies is often the one telling them. Gentle correction is important.
Deliberate lies	**Work**
Lies that are intentionally told to win the trust of others, for personal gain, to avoid problems, or to harm others.	Confront these lies directly. There will be fewer such lies when you work to prevent them. Create a culture where there is consensus that deliberate lies are unsuitable and socially unacceptable to both children and adults. The best way to repair the situation after a lie is for the person who has lied to recognise that he has done so.
Cover stories	**Work**
Refers to the types of lies told by people who have suffered serious neglect and/or traumatic events. These are lies that are not in line with reality, but contain elements of reality within them. They may be emotionally intense. They can be viewed as a way that the mind is connecting disjointed fragments of traumatic experiences.	Remember, it is not the child's intention to lie. One must gently return the orientation to reality. Remember that vulnerable and traumatised children are those telling these stories. Punishment and humiliation in front of others is not appropriate.

The dynamics of transgenerational trauma

Transgenerational trauma deals with the dynamics that lead traumatised parents to unwittingly infect their children with their traumas. It is important to be aware of this, as many vulnerable children are affected by their parents' traumatic stories. It may be difficult for the child to understand his own feelings, thoughts, and intentions, and it may be difficult for professionals working with a child who has not been directly traumatised to understand the child's behaviour.

The five phenomena described in the model are often seen in connection with transgenerational trauma (Hagelquist & Skov, 2014).

What to do?

You can use the list to analyse and understand the dynamics being experienced. The list can also be used to help professionals working with traumatised children understand children who have not been exposed to trauma but seem as if they have been infected by a parent's symptoms.

Tips and tricks

Establishing security before attempting to work with trauma also applies when working with transgenerational trauma.

Example

A woman talks about how her mother lived on the edge of starvation in Germany after the war. The woman has been affected by her mother's trauma in many ways, one of which is being extremely afraid of not having enough food. She draws lines on the bread, as her mother did, to keep an eye on how much her own daughter eats.

She also talks about her mother's need for quiet, and about how much she does not know about her mother's story. Both she and her daughter are horrified by the sound of thunder, which is a reminder of the bombings that her mother survived, even though they have not experienced the bombing themselves. The woman is working on not blindly imposing her mother's story onto her own daughter.

MODEL THE DYNAMICS OF TRANSGENERATIONAL TRAUMA

These five phenomena are often seen in connection with transgenerational trauma:

Repetition
Concerns that the child will be involved in or contribute to repeating some elements of the traumatic event.

Identification
Identification occurs when a child is constantly exposed to post-traumatic reactions from primary caregivers and begins to identify with those reactions and in some cases directly replays them through feelings, thoughts, or actions.

Silence
Silence is often experienced differently in families characterised by transgenerational trauma. The child in a traumatised family hears partial tales but silence about the family's history as a whole, especially when it involves stories associated with the trauma. Silence among the children of traumatised parents refers not only to silence in the larger historical context: silence is also a hallmark of the physical environment the child lives in. These children perceive their parents' vulnerability from their earliest ages and are raised to avoid making noise, provoke, or having loud conflicts inside the home.

Shame
Shame and trauma are closely interwoven. It is often the case that traumatised parents cause their children to feel shame. Shame is also closely interwoven with self-esteem. When parents feel ashamed and unworthy, it is difficult for them to support their child in feeling worthy and confident.

Immersion
Immersion refers to the dynamic where parents overwhelm the child by talking about traumatic experiences in graphic detail, leaving the child terrified.

Source: Hagelquist & Skov, 2014.

Chaos and rigidity

When regulating behaviour, there is a delicate balance between flexibility, chaos, and mentalizing on the one hand and limitations, boundaries, rigidity, and control on the other. The technique, as illustrated and inspired by Siegel and Bryson (2014), is to remain in the middle of the "river"; not too much chaos and flexibility, or, on the other hand, too rigid and behaviour-focused. Children (especially neglected and traumatised children) need structure, frames, and boundaries, but they also need life, moments of contact, mentalization, and flexibility.

What to do?

The picture on the next page illustrates the dilemma that you have as a caregiver when sailing the river and attempting to stay in the middle between the banks of chaos and rigidity. Some caregivers get too close to one bank. The chart can help you understand the importance of moving closer to the opposite bank to support a child's development. In some care environments, the two banks are represented by different people. The archetypal example is a family in which the father represents the side with boundaries, controls, and rigid rules, "He must learn that there are consequences when he misbehaves," while the mother represents the other bank with more chaos and flexibility, "He has had a bad day, so let it go just this once." The illustration can be used in connection with a mentalized conversation that shows the important elements of both banks.

Tips and tricks

Keep in mind that part of being a caregiver is working to stay in the middle of the river. If you are too much to the one side, work on moving towards the other. During a staff meeting, try encouraging the staff, who represent one bank, to experiment by taking and sticking to the other bank's perspective through a whole meeting.

Example

An institution has developed clear rules and regulations. Everyday life is manageable and predictable, and both the children and staff seem to thrive within the structure. A young woman attempts suicide and then refuses to go back to and expresses her unhappiness with the institution. The girl says that she is afraid of the staff and of violating the institution's many rules. She says that she misses adults who are interested in what is happening inside her. The institution gets a new leader who relaxes the rules, allowing for more life and chaos and giving the children more freedom. This allows for more interaction, but it also becomes clear to the staff that both children and adults are suffering from lack of structure and that things have become too chaotic. The model helps the staff understand that they must work towards being in the middle of the river.

Source: Siegel & Bryson 2014.

The victim–persecutor–rescuer triangle

Karpman (1968, 2007) described a psychological model of the dynamics activated in destructive interaction that can occur between people in conflict. The triangle has three positions or roles where one can be positioned. They are positions of interaction which the individual repeatedly has been accustomed to during his or her childhood and continues to occupy unconsciously throughout life, since they are predictable and therefore comfortable. One can say that it resembles a "game" where you unconsciously throw yourself into dramas as opposed to enduring your own discomfort (Hawkes, 2011).

What to do?

The victim–persecutor–rescuer triangle may be helpful in understanding which positions a child or adult, who has experience in engaging in such transactional positioning, places themselves and others in. It is non-mentalizing to predominantly position oneself as victim, rescuer, or persecutor. An example could be the fourteen-year-old girl who says: "You are ruining my life. The only one who can help me is my mother [rescuer], I have always been abused and betrayed [victim], and you are doing more of the same in this lousy institution [persecutor]." After a home visit she calls and says: "Come and get me, my mother is a total psychopath [persecutor]. It is good that you [rescuer] are there for me [victim]."

When mentalizing, one should attempt to find a nuanced position in the middle. Optimally, the girl would see that her mother can be supportive, but can also fail her and cause pain, just like an institution can be a place of support and comfort, but it can also be painful to be committed, and she herself can act out in ways that are both appropriate and inappropriate.

Tips and tricks

Examine the situations where the adolescent finds it difficult to understand without seeing himself as a victim in the triangle, and discuss that he is perhaps replaying the dance he has grown up with and that it is necessary to try to understand all the actors in the triangle in order to dissolve the patterns learned at home.

Example

A young woman experiences time and again that other people violate and deceive her. She is the victim in her personal relationships, her relationships with friends, at work, and with her family. During therapy, the victim–persecutor–rescuer triangle model is reviewed with her. It becomes clear that she spent much of her childhood trying to save her alcoholic mother, and that she often still feels victimised in relationships.

MODEL THE VICTIM–PERSECUTOR–RESCUER TRIANGLE

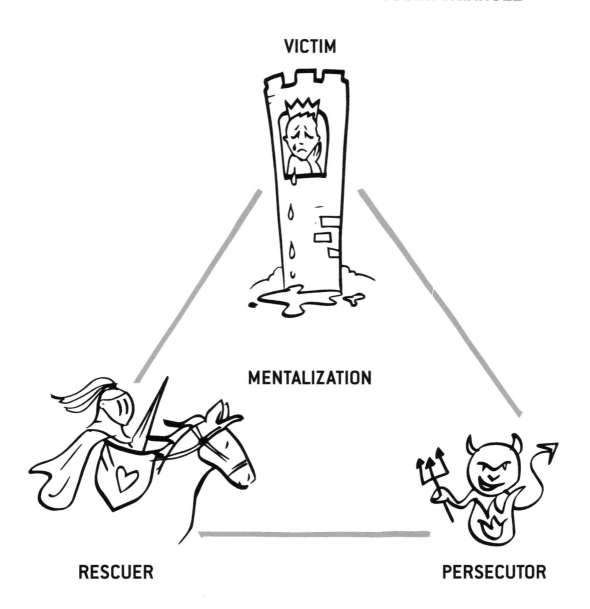

VICTIM

MENTALIZATION

RESCUER

PERSECUTOR

Part 3

TOOLS FOR THE PROFESSIONAL

Self reflection

As a professional, one must be able to put one's own mind at ease through mentalization, emotional regulation, and knowledge about one's own resources and triggers. This ability to reflect makes it possible for the professional to enter into relations that are stressful and emotionally straining in such a way that, despite challenges, he can still help the other person develop.

Knowledge of mirror neurons and parallel processes can explain why we are affected by other people's mental states and why we are affected in the interaction with people who are afraid, angry, powerless, and unhappy. This knowledge about how we are affected by others' emotions makes the need for reflecting upon one's own mental states (self-reflection) even more essential.

WHAT TO DO?

Working with vulnerable children and adolescents puts one at risk of being "infected" with a failure to mentalize and being overcome by intense emotions. The antidote against this is mentalization, reflection upon one's own mental states and finding inner calm. A great part of the work with one's own reflection is about the "here and now". Focus attention on using relaxation that allows for mentalization – even when emotions are at their highest. In "times of peace" it's important to attend to building up skills to calm oneself and regulate emotions. It can be a good idea regularly to do some of the exercises from this part of the guide to become better at mentalizing in the here and now.

TIPS AND TRICKS

Use the models in this part of the guide to measure your own emotional intensity and ability to mentalize. Grow accustomed to using some of the models (for example, the temperature gauge) before having difficult conversations with vulnerable children or adolescents.

EXAMPLE

A youth worker is on her way to a conversation with an adolescent who has told a lie about another adolescent. This lie has had serious consequences. The youth worker remembers the temperature gauge model about working with her own ability to mentalize and reflect. In this way she realises that this is one of the situations that has often gone wrong for her. She asks a colleague to handle the conversation instead.

The OPEN thermometer

When interacting with people exhibiting strong emotions, it is the professional's task to function as a kind of thermostat that sets the desired emotional temperature. This makes the professional a role model who shows that emotional states can be regulated through reflection. It is also important to be aware of when, as a professional, you can no longer engage in a development enhancing interaction. In those circumstances you can enlist the father and mother, or possibly swap with a colleague who is not so emotional and is able to mentalize in the situation.

What to do?
Let the OPEN temperature gauge be the tool you use in the moment to assess whether you are able to enter into a mentalizing interaction.

Tips and tricks
Using the model shortly after a difficult situation where your ability to mentalize has failed can help you be aware of how you feel and experience, when you are capable of self-reflection and when you are not. Start by using the model on paper, but transfer it along the way to be an automatic gauge when emotions are running high.

Example
A family therapist is getting ready to confront a colleague and tell her how frustrated she is over what she feels was unprofessional work her colleague engaged in during a home visit to a family they work with together. Just before she steps into the room, she measures her "temperature" to gauge whether her mind is OPEN enough for such a conversation.

MODEL THE OPEN THERMOMETER

What is my emotional temperature on a scale of 1–10?_____

Am I *open* to seeing things from multiple perspectives?_____

Is there a *balance* between the need to take action and reflection?_____

Am I able to feel *empathy* for both myself and the others involved?_____

Am I sincerely *curious* about the mental states behind the behaviour?_____

Do I have the time and *patience* to do this properly?_____

The three questions

The book *No-drama Discipline* (Siegel & Bryson, 2014) tackles how to create peace and self-reflection and set limits in a way that will create learning and simultaneously develop a child's mentalization ability. It specifies that "discipline" originally meant to teach or give instruction and that this is exactly what discipline is about – to teach the child what it is not yet capable of and not to punish him.

What to do?

When you are in a situation where the child is testing the boundaries or is having a mentalization failure, think "why? – what? – how?":
Why is he doing this now?
What does he need me to teach him?
How can I teach him what he needs?
It then becomes a question of **"will" or "can"**. "Will" he not? Or "can" he not?

Tips and tricks

Learning and using the "why? – what? – how?" method can help to avoid falling into the trap of mentalization failure.

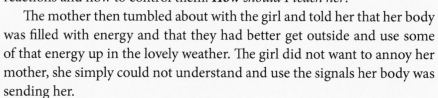

Example

A girl has recently been ill, and when she got well, she kept jumping on her mother, making loud noises, and knocking things over. First the mother thought: "This child needs discipline!" Then she thought of the above advice on regulating strong emotions and "discipline". *Why is my daughter acting like this?* Because she has been inside for days and is now healthy and full of energy. *What do I need to teach her?* To understand her body's reactions and how to control them. *How should I teach her?*

The mother then tumbled about with the girl and told her that her body was filled with energy and that they had better get outside and use some of that energy up in the lovely weather. The girl did not want to annoy her mother, she simply could not understand and use the signals her body was sending her.

Inspired by Siegel & Bryson, 2014

The breathing space

The "breathing space" is one of the basic exercises in a mindfulness-based stress coping programme developed by the American doctor Jon Kabat-Zinn. The programme has gained wide popularity over the past twenty years. It is a way to strengthen the ability to maintain an Open mind through mindfulness exercises. The most basic of these exercises is "breathing space", which typically lasts for three to five minutes.

What to do?

The breathing space is a simple exercise that can be used as often as needed. It offers a quick and effective way to focus attention and create a conscious presence. The instructions for the exercise are on the next page.

Tips and tricks

When doing the exercise for the first few times, it is probably most effective to have some kind of guide (look for an app, for example). After a few weeks of daily practice, you will be able to do the exercise on your own whenever you need to be more present and find a better balance. Over time, your ability to spontaneously do the breathing space exercise will become an integral part of your coping mechanism.

It is natural for the mind to wander, especially in the middle phase of the exercise. Every time you find yourself lost, practise gently bringing yourself back to the breathing space.

Example

A head of department has just been involved in an incident where two adolescents in her section were involved in a fight. She has to leave the situation to an employee to go to an important meeting with a mother and a case worker. On the way to the meeting, she realises that she is too upset to be properly present. She walks past the case worker's office first and finds a quiet place to do the breathing space exercise. After completing the exercise, she feels ready for the upcoming meeting.

Note: This exercise was developed in collaboration with Jeppe Budde.

MODEL THE BREATHING SPACE

Sit somewhere where you can be at peace.

It is essential that you find a setting characterised by openness, curiosity, and acceptance, so you do not have to try to change or control what you observe.

Start by noticing your BODY: the contact with the ground and areas of pleasantness and unpleasantness.

Similarly, notice your MIND: the thoughts, moods, or feelings that are present in the moment.

Now notice the SOUNDS that surround you: the sounds inside you, the sounds in the room, and the sounds outside the room.

After some time, narrow your focus and concentrate on how the spontaneous breathing relaxes your body.

At the end of the exercise, reopen your consciousness to the sounds, mind, and body and the wholeness of the moment.

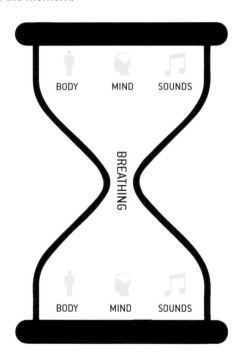

Mentalizing failure and self-reflection

Mentalization fails when you lose focus on your own mental states and the mental states of others. Simply, you lose track of your own feelings, needs, goals, reasons, and thoughts, and those of others involved.

A mentalization failure occurs when the professional blocks out the other person's mental state in order to handle the strong emotions and sense of powerlessness she is experiencing.

What to do?

Fill out the questionnaire on the following three pages. You can make this exercise part of supervision or teaching, but it is also a good idea to do it several times after difficult situations that arise in your own work.

Tips and tricks

If the model is applied shortly after a difficult situation where your own ability to mentalize collapsed, it may help show where it failed.

> ### Example
> A teacher does the exercise after a conflict with her teenage daughter. While doing the exercise it becomes clear that it is much harder for her to deal with conflicts at home than when she is in the field working with troubled teens. She is also aware that the same themes make it hard for her to mentalize both at work and in her private life. She becomes conscious of the themes she should be aware of and focus on, and what she can bring from her work that she can also use at home. She is also aware that the part of mentalization psychology that states again and again that mentalizing is most difficult in relations with those that we have strong feelings for, applies very much to her own life.

MODEL QUESTIONNAIRE FOR WORK WITH MENTALIZING FAILURE AND SELF-REFLECTION

Consider a challenging situation where you felt that your mentalization ability failed. It should be a recent situation with either your own child or a child/adolescent that you work with.

Give a short description of the situation:

_____

_____

How did you feel?

_____

_____

What were you thinking?

_____

_____

What was happening in your body?

_____

_____

What did you do?

_____

_____

_____

_____

How do you feel when you think about the situation now? Feelings, thoughts, needs for taking action, and bodily reactions?

_____

_____

_____

Is there something about the situation that is particularly difficult for you? A trigger that may also occur in other situations: for example, behaviours that are reminiscent of former experiences or your own mental state: weariness, sadness, or stress?

_____

_____

_____

Are there any of your reactions that are typical for you when you feel stressed or provoked?

_____

_____

_____

Look at your answers to the previous questions and circle what might be a sign to you in future situations. These elements – whether they be elements of the situation or your own reactions – are signs that can help you to take care of yourself. Being aware of what triggers you will help you act on it.

Think of situations where you feel stressed, provoked, or otherwise experience a high level of emotional intensity. What do you do to calm yourself in these situations? It could be, for example: working on staying calm, breathing techniques, trying to keep the focus on the mental state of yourself and the other person, remaining present mentally, trying to get through the situation until it is over, asking for help, etc.

_____

_____

_____

Reflection on situations when you feel stressed, provoked, or otherwise experience high emotional intensity:

Before:
Try to find a number of coping strategies that you can use before you go into the situation. Write them down. Coping strategies can help you be prepared for the situation, for example, when you will be going into a room where a fifteen-year-old girl is very angry and throwing things. There can also be relaxation strategies and support from others.

_____

_____

_____

During:
Strategies you can make use of during the situation, for example: breathing, muscle relaxation, or a personal mantra. Include strategies you can use to prevent a relapse of mentalization failure. What strategies can you use to prevent attempting to repair conflicts until the emotional intensity has fallen and how can you continue attempting to mentalize?

_____

_____

_____

After:
What recovery strategies can you use? For example, reflection upon the mental state you and the child/adolescent were in that gave rise to your and the child's behaviour. Do something fun together and restore contact.

_____

_____

_____

Inspired by Blaustein & Kinniburgh, 2010

Pseudo-mentalization

When we as professionals are emotionally pressured by a child's or adolescent's inappropriate behaviour, we can easily begin to pseudo-mentalize. Pseudo-mentalization feels and sounds like mentalizing, but is characterised by a tendency to express certainty without acknowledging the uncertainties associated with knowing about someone else's mind: that minds are separate and that mental states are opaque. This means that you never completely know how another person thinks or feels (Bateman & Fonagy, 2012, p. 516).

What to do?

Try to remember a time when you had a definite and cocksure, perhaps negative idea of what was going on in a child's mind. Determine if there were special circumstances at play and consider whether there is a risk that if you find yourself in similar circumstances you would be apt to start pseudo-mentalizing.

Tips and tricks

Try to think of pseudo-mentalizing in different contexts in relation to a partner, a friend, your children, or other family members.

Example

An eight-year-old boy is being placed in an institution. The boy is very adult and wants to be involved in all decisions – both for himself and for the other children in the institution. The staff meet and agree that his need for control should not be encouraged. When the staff works with pseudo-mentalization, it is precisely this boy that comes to several of their minds. There could be many reasons for the boy's behaviour and his need to be in control of his life. In his home, there was no one else to take control when he lived alone with his alcoholic mother. He has also set a goal to be a good and helpful boy. He has a fear of completely losing control if he lets adults make decisions. He also tries to do the things that he believes adults will have him do.

PSEUDO-MENTALIZATION IN PRACTICE

Examples of pseudo-mentalization:

"She is lazy"
"He's resisting"
"He is manipulative"
"He is taking cheap shots"
"She wants to control us"
"She just doesn't want to"
"He doesn't care"
"He just wants attention"
"She wants to have the last say in everything"
"He is provoking"
"It's his ADHD that's talking"

Have you encountered pseudo-mentalization?

_____

_____

_____

Have you been in situations where you pseudo-mentalized in relation to a child?

_____

_____

_____

Do you remember if there was a reason that you pseudo-mentalized in the situation – for example, that you were emotionally pressured, or that you were too busy to consider the mental state behind the child's behaviour, or ...

_____

_____

_____

Inspired by Fonagy & Allison, 2012

Paths to maintaining reflection and calm with balance and support

Reflection and tranquillity are necessary for creating a productive interaction. It is often reflection from the professional that is lacking. The professional may feel that he has to act in the situation, and the adolescent then feels that the professional is reacting without reflection, but instead with stress, anger, verbal outbursts, or power plays. This is simply "more wood on the fire".

The professional should instead act as a kind of thermostat to adjust the desired emotional temperature. The professional also becomes a role model, showing that emotional states can be adjusted through reflection.

Without reflection, it is impossible to provide marked mirroring, and thus not possible to provide the proper support for the regulation of emotions. When encountering intense, unregulated emotions, one can easily become affected by these feelings, and anxiety or anger can diminish one's ability to reflect. Taking care of oneself is vital for maintaining one's own ability to reflect during the often personally demanding job of working with neglected and traumatised people. The model helps maintain awareness of how important it is that professionals take care of themselves and know where to find comfort at work through colleagues and how to best look after themselves.

What to do?
Sometimes it's a good idea to fill in a model like the one on the next page when things are calm to learn how to take care of yourself and your ability to reflect.

Tips and tricks
Filling in the model helps the professional realise that social work is demanding and that we often use ourselves as "tools", so we need service and support to stay strong for a long time and continue to mentalize.

> ### Example
> A family counsellor uses the model to help her focus on the things she has forgotten that help her create a balance between work and leisure in her life. She says, "I never seem to get in better shape no matter how much I run." A colleague says, "A long time ago I told myself, that if I am to be able to handle this, I have to learn that I cannot 'work my way out of my work.'"

MODEL QUESTIONNAIRE FOR WORKING TO MAINTAIN REFLECTION AND CALM DURING DIFFICULT INTERACTIONS

Working with neglected and traumatised children and adolescents can be exhausting and isolating. How can I get support from my colleagues?

_____

_____

_____

Organisations that help these children depend on our efforts. How can I get support from my organisation and other organisations?

_____

_____

_____

Our workload can be overwhelming. How can I balance my personal workload?

_____

_____

_____

Work has a tendency to interfere with and invade our private lives. How can I maintain boundaries between my work and my private life?

_____

_____

_____

Interacting with traumatised children and adolescents can activate traumatic material from our own lives. How can I find help coping with those themes?

_____

_____

_____

How can I create space for breaks, recreation, creativity, and make sure I take care of myself?

_____

_____

_____

Inspired by Blaustein & Kinniburgh, 2010

Part 4

EXERCISES

The last part of the guide consists of a large number of exercises which can be used with the child, the adolescent, or with their families. The exercises are divided according to the STORM model, so they start with the Security theme and thereafter Think trauma. Afterwards, there are a number of exercises to help in Obtaining the skills: emotions, behaviour, attention/cognition, physique, sense of self, and relationships. Then there are a number of exercises dealing with Resources. Finally, there are exercises for training the ability to mentalize.

WHAT TO DO?

Use the exercises as they appear or as an inspiration to develop your own exercises, or develop them further with those you work with.

TIPS AND TRICKS

Copy and collect the exercises you do with a child in a folder. The folder will make your work feel more tangible. It will also give the child a chance to see his development history when the therapy is finished. It can be used as a transitional object when the relationship ends. Many of the children and families involved in this kind of work are not accustomed to receiving gifts, so think of ways to make the folder special – aesthetics and generosity are also ethics.

EXAMPLE

A mother is alone with four children, who each have a number of diagnoses. She meets with the different authorities and the network concerning her children. She also goes to family counselling, but she cries all the time so her therapist has a hard time using the Mentalization Guide with the mother and her children, even though there appear to be a lot of skills that need to be developed. Her family therapist is fortunately aware that a sense of security for the mother and family are most important, and that the therapist maintains a relationship where the mother can share how overburdened she is. Along the way, the family has fun doing the exercises without experiencing them as just another programme they have to take part in.

Security – creating security

There is broad agreement within the trauma field that offering a sense of security is crucial to helping a child (Allen, Fonagy, & Bateman, 2010; Herman, 1995; Levine & Kline, 2007; Perry & Szalavitz, 2011). Offering a traumatised child or adolescent security may seem banal, but it is fundamental. Parents and professionals can easily forget to do the most necessary and natural things when they have a new child in their care. The central part of treatment is to offer the child a relationship and an environment in which he feels safe.

What to do?

When you have time to prepare to help a traumatised child, it is a good idea to tailor the treatment in relation to the individual child's and family's needs. Even a lot of preparation does not change the fact that the professional should be meeting the child with an Open mind and work towards establishing security at the first meeting and in all future interactions. Focus should be on the environment surrounding the child and the child's sense of security within his network. Focusing on past trauma here is equally central. It is also important to focus on the organisation and employees who will work with the child to ensure that they are mentalized in an environment where they feel safe.

Tips and tricks

When working with children and adolescents who have experienced repeated trauma from their primary caregivers, security is a recurring theme. It is important to take this seriously and not see it as an interruption of treatment. Working with traumatic children, it can be the treatment in itself.

> ### Example
> A six-year-old girl arrives at a residential institution. The staff have prepared for her arrival in a wide range of areas. These include making sure that the same educator is at work continuously from the first time she's there. The girl will be able to decorate her own room, and the staff will listen to what she likes to eat and to her need for contact with her mother.

MODEL CREATING SECURITY

- Unique mentalization in relation to the specific child

- The child is met with an Open mind – Openness, Balance, Empathy, Curiosity, Patience

- Security for the child based on an everyday rhythm and rituals

- Preparing for what will happen both in the short term and in the long run

- The adults send non-verbal signals to the child that, "I am interested in you, and I wish you well"

- The adults signal honesty and transparency

- The physical environment indicates to the child that he is important. The child's room/environment is age-appropriate – and preferably designed in interaction with the child

- The adults relate to the child's living conditions, concerns about litigation, school location, home visits

- If the child is still in danger, a security plan should be developed. A security plan should be a specific plan for what the child can do if his security is threatened (the telephone number of the case worker, the contact person, and direct action instructions on what the child should do in the event of danger)

- Establishing a secure, collaborative environment around the child (where parents, foster parents, case workers, school teachers, and school psychologist all work together)

- The staff must feel that they are part of a secure organisation where there is a focus on mentalizing and security for the organisation and staff

Security – treating stress

When the nervous system is stressed, it is important for the feeling of security. Therefore, it is a good idea to pay attention to relaxing the nervous system. This model simply provides a number of ideas for how to work to support a nervous system that is under stress. There are ideas for acute stress, and tips for working long-term with a stressed nervous system.

What to do?

Use the model as inspiration to help a person whose nervous system is under stress.

Tips and tricks

Remember that when the nervous system is affected by stress, the ability to mentalize and learn is limited, so it is important to employ the strategies from the model.

Example

A ten-year-old boy comes back to school after a summer holiday where he should have visited his grandparents in Gaza. Israel has sent ground troops into Gaza, making the visit impossible. The boy constantly sits at home and watches images from the war zone on TV and on Facebook. He is in a highly emotional state and very stressed. He needs his teacher to seriously consider how he can help the boy ease his alertness and stress.

MODEL IDEAS FOR TREATING STRESS

- Consolation

- Hugs

- Quiet movements and voices

- Body contact

- Joyful moments

- Singing and rhythm

- Photos of relatives or other persons cared for

- Visible routes of escape

- Soothing music

- Holding hands

- Hand on chest and hand on stomach

- Anticipating change

- Divertion

- Relaxation exercises

- Breathing exercises (e.g., breathe in for a count of five, hold your breath for a count of six, exhale for a count of seven)

- Mindfulness

- Meditation

- Diet

- Exercise

- "Butterfly hug" (where you hug yourself and flap yourself on the arms)

- Good sleep routine

- Time

Inspired by Jørgensen & Hagmund-Hansen, 2013

Security – angels in the nursery

"Angels in the nursery" are the positive subjects/stories remembered about childhood. Our angels in the nursery are mental images of people who have wished us well. These can be used to provide security by bringing them out and remembering them.

The angels in the nursery may be people who were caring and loving or helped out at a difficult moment in childhood. People who held on when everything seemed impossible, or people who have seen the worst of one's behaviour and still loved you unconditionally.

What to do?

The model can be used with children, adolescents, or families, but it is also good for the professional to fill out. Instruct your child to fill in the angel with drawings or words about people who have been particularly significant.

Tips and tricks

Angels can also be religious figures or animals. When you ask for angels, you may have to help the child find the people who helped him discover that it is valuable to change.

> **Example**
> A boy remembers his late grandmother and what she did to help him retain faith in himself.

MODEL **YOUR ANGEL**

Security – sleep

When the body does not get enough rest at night it is hard to function during the day. Difficulties with sleep are common following trauma and often seen in traumatised children and adolescents.

A lack of rest in the body and mind is significant in a number of areas. It can lead to fatigue, irritability, learning difficulties, and increased stress. Sleep is included in the STORM model, because a body and mind deprived of sleep lack a basic sense of security.

What to do?

The suggestions for improving sleep can be used with children, adolescents, or families where sleeping is a problem. The most important thing is to take sleep problems seriously and try to test strategies tailored to the individual. In the model, the frameworks for better sleep are mentioned first because they are very important for getting a good night's sleep. For example, having fixed waking times and bedtimes and avoiding activities that increase alertness, and instead engaging in quiet activities. Take steps to establish regular sleeping habits for both adolescents and adults. The rest of the ideas can be tested and adjusted to the individual.

Tips and tricks

Be alert and mentalize in relation to the individual person. For some, MusiCure (www.musicure.com), developed by Niels Eje, is a great help. It is music designed to calm the nervous system. Others will find it annoying. One should also be aware that some children and adolescents who have experienced severe trauma need to have the television on because silence can trigger trauma.

Example

A sixteen-year-old boy has great difficulty sleeping. Some nights he doesn't sleep at all. The boy has had sleep problems for most of his life. He experienced that marijuana helps him sleep, but in the long run, it aggravates his sleep problems. He is fighting to re-establish a regular circadian rhythm. His teacher talks to him about what to do. The boy says, sadly: "I have a messed up circadian rhythm and I hate to go to bed, because all I do is think. The only thing that works is marijuana." The teacher and the boy study the list. Testing one solution after another is a long and difficult process, but knowing that the teacher takes the boy's sleep problem seriously helps to create a special relationship and as time goes on, the boy finds a better rhythm and sleeps easier.

MODEL **SLEEP**

- A good sleep rhythm – wake up and go to sleep at the same time every day – independent of sleep
- Exercise
- Mindfulness
- Bedtime rituals
- Talk about or write down concerns well before bedtime
- Relaxing music, such MusiCure, available as an app
- A warm bath before bedtime
- Massage
- Comfortable duvet
- Yawn (it really works)
- Count backwards from 1000
- Valerian tablets (a herbal remedy, but be aware of age limits)
- Warm milk with honey before bedtime (an old folk remedy, but it could help)
- Relaxation exercises
- Relaxation exercises recorded by the primary caregiver
- Breathing exercises (breathe in, count to five, hold your breath for a count of six, exhale for a count of seven)
- Have a variety of soothing thoughts, such as: "It is quite common not to be able to sleep," "The body can manage with less sleep," or "I do relaxation exercises so my body can also relax"
- Research whether the sleep enhancer melatonin is needed

Inspired by Akasha & Olsen, 2006

Security – exercise for falling asleep

Traumatised children and adolescents often have difficulty getting rest and sleep. They can have difficulty falling asleep and then wake up an hour and a half after they fell asleep, unable to fall asleep again. The child may feel very frightened when he is alone at night. Some children have had traumatic experiences at night, or they have experienced being hit or assaulted while in bed.

What to do?

Before using this exercise, make sure that none of the words could trigger discomfort. The word "stairs", for example. Instead of stairs, choose "lift", "a long walk", or "a wooded path". If you are working with a small child, he can bring along a cuddly toy or something similar. It is also possible to enlist an assistant to help with the exercise. You should also make sure that the child knows all the body parts used in the exercise. Does the child know what "groin" is, for example? In other words, adjust your language to match the child's knowledge and vocabulary.

Expect that it will take time before the child catches on and realises that the technique is working. Be prepared for the child to open his eyes, laugh, and toss and turn in bed during the exercise. Also expect the child to comment on your voice. He may think you are talking "strangely" and using a different voice than you do in everyday conversation. Be patient and realise that you will have to repeat the exercise several times.

The exercise should be done in a calm voice which becomes slower and softer as the exercise progresses. It is important that you speak slowly. Make sure that the child has a chance to follow your suggestions.

Customise the exercise to the adolescents you work with, make sure words like "ball" or "stairs" create positive associations, rather than triggering something negative. Customise the exercise to the child's breathing. Check to see if the child has latched on to the idea of the ball, stairs, or the breathing. Repeat everything in your own words. It is important that your words and phrases be invitations – not orders.

Tips and tricks

Record the exercise on a sound file so the child can listen to it on his own. This is a way of supporting the child at being independent in providing his own reassurance at falling asleep.

The exercise can also be given to the child's parents, so they can use it to help the child fall asleep.

Example

An eight-year-old girl lived with her critically ill mother when her sickness was at its worst. During the worst periods of her sickness, the mother could be aggressive and violent towards her when the disease made her see her daughter as a dangerous animal. While with her foster family, the girl suffers from nightmares and is afraid to fall asleep. Her foster father sits with her every night and uses a calm voice to help her fall asleep.

MODEL EXERCISE FOR FALLING ASLEEP

Lie down and rest as comfortably as you can. Your eyes can be open or closed, it's up to you. Feel the way your bed and your body touch each other. I do not know what you are feeling — perhaps it's the warmth of the mattress — or perhaps a feeling of support. Maybe you feel the duvet over you or around you. Give yourself some time to feel what it is like to lie here in your bed with your duvet around you.

While in your bed, comforted by your duvet and mattress (and perhaps a cuddly toy), breathe deeply. Breathe deeply through your nose. Feel how the breath comes in through your nose, travels into your lungs and comes out through the mouth. (Keep an eye on the child and say "nice" or "good" or "well done" when you can see that the child is breathing deeply. Make sure that any adults present breathe in the same way, so that the child will be able to hear them breathing and feel supported).

While you take another deep breath, you can — if you have not already done so — close your eyes. Breathe deeply again. Feel yourself relaxing more and more.

Imagine, however you'd like, a small ball. Feel warm. Maybe it has a colour, maybe not. Imagine that the ball is rolling around and around. Around and around in gentle movements. Breathe deeply while imagining the ball. Maybe you see it, maybe you just feel it, either way is fine. However you imagine the ball is OK.

Now imagine that the ball is inside your body. It is a pleasant and nice ball. It moves softly around and around. Wherever the ball is inside your body feels calm and relaxed. Imagine the ball gently running around your head. Slowly. Slowly and pleasantly. Slowly and softly. Feel your head becoming calm and relaxed.

The ball rolls on. Out into your shoulders. You are already feeling warm, calm, and relaxed. The ball rolls on. Out into one arm. Out into the other arm. Through the upper body, into your abdomen, lower back, legs, knees, feet, all the way out to your toes. Wherever the ball is and wherever it has been feels more and more relaxed. The ball is a relaxation ball.

Now, breathe deeply into your entire body — feel yourself relax more and more.

Now, any way you choose, imagine a staircase. You choose how it looks, but it's a nice staircase. A fine staircase. A staircase you feel comfortable with. Maybe it is a specific colour, maybe it has a handrail. Perhaps it's short, perhaps it's long. Perhaps there are many steps, maybe a few. Whatever you see is fine. The stairs are cozy and comfortable.

Now imagine that you are standing at the top of the stairs. Quietly begin to go down the stairs. One step at a time. Perhaps you stop and take stock of your feelings. The staircase is safe and comfortable. Breathe deeply and take another step. And another. Breathe deeply from your abdomen and feel yourself becoming more and more relaxed. And more and more relaxed. Step by step. You begin to feel tired. It spreads through your body as peace and tranquillity. Step by step, down the stairs.

All the way down the stairs … third step … fourth … fifth … sixth … seventh … eighth … ninth … tenth …

Good night and sweet dreams …

Trauma focus – the survivor knight

Traumatic events have a profound effect on the person who experiences them. They can result in a wide range of post-traumatic reactions. When a child is traumatised by his primary caregivers he experiences the feeling of being abandoned mentally.

Working with trauma is a balancing act, where the child's boundaries must not be exceeded by attempting to articulate and work with trauma too quickly. On the other hand, being overly cautious in talking about trauma leaves the adolescent alone with the trauma.

Remember that trauma treatment is: "A secure attachment context conducive to mentalizing in which previously unbearable emotional states can be experienced, expressed, understood and reflected upon – and thereby rendered meaningful and bearable" (Allen, 2013, p. 33).

What to do?
When working with trauma, the following four points are important:

1. Creating a trauma-informed environment

2. That the child will be informed about trauma (see Part 2 on psycho-education)

3. That the child will be assisted in seeing himself positively and as one who has mastered his trauma the best possible way

4. Working to overcome the avoidance of the trauma that has created fear (often in collaboration with a psychologist)

The model can be used with points 2 and 3 to support the child in understanding that it is quite common for trauma to have a profound effect on children, and that he has actually done something right in the trauma situation.

Tips and tricks
If the child perceives that the illustrations are childish, show the drawing and say that it is used in working with children. Tell him that it is important to "trauma focus" because children typically do not talk about what they have experienced, but it still takes up space inside because they feel that they have done something wrong and they have not moved on. You can also say that children often do not see that they have done anything good, and often even feel guilty, even though it is not their fault that they were beaten, that their car crashed, or that their sister was ill. These children need to learn to see themselves as a "survival knight". The conversation may lead to the child speaking about his own traumatic experience and how he mastered the situation.

Example

A thirteen-year-old boy listens with interest to his psychologist telling him to "trauma focus" and be the "survival knight". He says: "It's strange that I feel that it was my fault and I keep thinking about all the violence that my mother and my siblings were exposed to and that I did not do anything to stop it. I don't feel the same way about my little sister. I think she did everything right and it is terrible that she still thinks about it. Perhaps I could also think about myself that way."

MODEL THE SURVIVOR KNIGHT

Most children who have survived trauma experience doubt as to whether they did the right thing — they overlook the many small positive things they did during the difficult time. Do you think/can you find any such examples of good things, that you did?

_____

_____

Many children find it difficult to spot the good they accomplished. But if a completely different child experienced what you have been through, how would you feel about that child?

_____

_____

Trauma focus – trigger analysis

Reacting to danger triggers a person's alarm system. This alarm system is a good thing and has helped human beings survive through the ages. When the alarm goes off, it prepares the body to react to danger. It gives us the energy to fight, flee, or freeze. It enables us to respond to danger. Once we have experienced a dangerous situation, we will be on guard when we encounter the same triggers again. Sometimes, though, it can be a false alarm – for example, when we hear, see, or feel something that reminds us of a past experience (Blaustein & Kinniburgh, 2010).

What to do?

Trigger-analysis is used to analyse a particular situation from the child's perspective. What was the specific behaviour? Which internal triggers (feelings, thoughts, etc.), and external triggers (the behaviour of others, smells, sounds, etc.) precipitated the behaviour? What emotions did the child experience and what are the reasons behind the behaviour?

Trigger-analysis can also be used from the adult's perspective.

Tips and tricks

Overall, it's a good idea to keep the child away from his triggers. Work can be done to eventually overcome the child's fear of triggers. That requires that you first know the triggers.

Example

An eleven-year-old girl overreacts when she feels she is being treated unfairly. Something as simple as a soda being shared with another child can be a trigger. She can start to punch, kick, and pull hair and is unable to let go of her anger, fear, and sadness.

The girl has experienced that her stepfather favoured his biological child and purposefully humiliated her. She was, for example, made to sit on a kitchen tile and was not allowed to step outside the tile while her sister played and enjoyed herself. Trigger-analysis made it clear to both the teacher and the girl that her brain is triggered when she thinks she is being unjustly treated.

Note: The exercise was created in cooperation with psychologist Line Sangild Thimmer.

MODEL **TRIGGER ANALYSIS**

Trigger inner/ outer [What triggered the behaviour? What happened?]	Behaviour [Description of behavior. What did you do?]	Emotions [What emotions did you experience?]	Reasons [What were the reasons for reacting the way you did?]

Trauma focus – the 90/10 response

When the brain has been exposed to something extremely unpleasant or trauma, it perceives the present differently emotionally. The brain experiences, senses, and catalogues experiences that are happening "here and now" based 90 per cent on what happened in the past and only 10 per cent on what is happening here and now (Allen, Fonagy, & Bateman, 2010). It could be a child who has been trapped in a fire who then has an extreme reaction when a roll of paper towels catches fire while he is at home with his foster family. He runs out, screaming and crying and it takes a long time to comfort him afterwards.

The brain often reacts with fear or anger in harmless situations where something reminds it of the past. This happens to protect the child from being exposed to the trauma again.

What to do?

Describe the 90/10 reaction to the child. Explain that it is common when you have experienced something dangerous to experience the world as if you are back in that situation. The task is to learn to tell the difference between the present and the past. Work to get the percentage down to 80/20 and eventually even smaller.

Tips and tricks

Remember 90/10 responses are not intentional. It is stressful for the person experiencing the response – as well as for those around them.

Example

A teacher is sitting at the bedside of a girl who has been sexually assaulted. When he gives her a goodnight hug, her entire body tenses up. When he leaves, the girl calls her contact person and says that the teacher abused her. The girl experienced the situation as if she was being abused again. She is seeing only 10 per cent of the reality she is experiencing here and now and 90 per cent of the previous trauma.

MODEL THE 90/10 RESPONSE: THE BRAIN READS THE WORLD AS IF IT IS STILL DANGEROUS

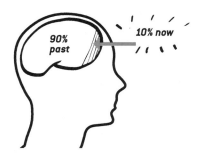

Do you know examples, where your brain was reacting as if you were back in the bad situation?

_____

_____

Can you feel the difference between then and now? Does it feel totally like you are in the past, or are there parts of your brain that know that you are not back there?

_____

_____

Draw what and how much the past, relative to the present, fills your brain when you are under stress.

How can you teach your brain that the past is the past and the present is the present?

_____

_____

Trauma focus – the brain's alarm system

Everyone has a built-in alarm system, which signals when we are in danger and prepares us to respond to that danger. When one has been exposed to trauma, the alarms become extra sensitive and often go off when there is no danger because something recalls the previous trauma. These are called triggers. It is important that those around the child recognise these triggers so they can understand the child's reaction and understand why his alarm system was triggered (Blaustein & Kinniburgh, 2010). Discussing the trigger is a way to let the child know that he is experiencing a natural reaction to a traumatic experience, and it can help relatives restore confidence and calm when they understand the cause of the child's reaction.

What to do?

Describe to the child how the brain's alarm system works and fill in the model on the following page together.

The thinking brain: When we feel safe and comfortable, we are calm enough to think rational thoughts. When we are calm, we are able to say and do things we know are good for us and fit with how we would like to see ourselves. The thinking brain sorts out what is real danger and what is a false alarm.

The alarmed brain: The brain sends a signal when there is danger, so we can act on it or escape from it. This can be very helpful, for example, if we are about to be hit by a car or attacked by a wild animal. Danger signals are generated both from intuition and the dangerous situations we have experienced in our lifetime. Sometimes the brain sends a false alarm. This could be when we see, hear or feel something that reminds us of an ugly experience. These reminders are called triggers. The brain has learned to recognise the triggers we have experienced when we have been in danger. We all have unique danger signals that set our alarms in motion. What triggers these alarms varies from person to person.

The affected brain: When the alarms in our brain are activated, our affected brain is set in motion. The brain prepares the body to act by creating extra energy so we can either get away quickly or defend ourselves. This is vital when there is real danger, like a car coming straight at us, but it is less desirable when it's a false alarm and there is no real danger. The affected brain may cause us to do something that we'll come to regret.

Tips and tricks

The adult can help the child fill out "the thinking brain" in the model and point out the times when the child has been a good friend, creative, caring, and a team player.

Example

A boy is sitting in class and reading. A friend beside him drops his ruler on the floor. It is very quiet in the classroom, so it sounds very loud when the ruler hits the floor. The boy hits his classmate on the side of the head with his school bag.

The brain model is helpful when the teacher subsequently talks with the boy about the incident. The boy says he was totally absorbed by the story he was reading. He is an accomplished reader (the thinking brain), but he was actually very influenced by the mother in the story losing her hair because his own mother lost her hair as he and his family were fleeing from the war. When the loud noise happened, his brain threw a switch (alarmed brain) causing him to hit his friend (affected brain).

The model can help the boy understand himself, and help the teacher talk to the boy about the incident and how he could respond differently if a similar situation arises.

Note: The exercise was prepared in cooperation with psychologist Line Sangild Thimmer.

MODEL THE BRAIN'S ALARM SYSTEM

The thinking brain	How do you view yourself in good times? When you feel calm, safe, and are doing well?
	_____ _____ _____ _____ _____ _____
The alarmed brain	What triggers your brain to enter a state of alarm? What triggers your brain before it enters an alarmed state?
	_____ _____ _____ _____ _____ _____
The affected brain	How does your brain react when it acts without thinking?
	_____ _____ _____ _____ _____ _____

Trauma focus – re-enactment

Re-enactment is when a child reacts to a traumatic experience by constantly putting himself in the same or a similar situation and re-enacting the trauma. Sometimes it happens because the child is trying to understand something that has previously been incomprehensible. Sometimes it happens because the child wants to gain control over something that he had no control over when it happened. It is important to note that children often do not even realise why they are re-enacting the unpleasant situation. Repeating a traumatic experience is an expression of the fact that the trauma is not yet an integrated part of the traumatised self-understanding and a wish for such an integration.

Re-enactment often places the child in new unpleasant situations and rarely helps the child to understand the initial situation. Re-enactment thus becomes a vicious cycle, preventing the child from understanding the trauma or his self in light of the trauma, which begins to loom larger and exert more influence over the child's life.

Re-enactment can make someone feel very alone, and instead of getting closer to an understanding, a child often finds himself in new and unpleasant situations, which the caregivers can have difficulties understanding; they might even be angry and repel the child.

One way to counter re-enactments is to provide a secure place where mentalization allows previously unbearable experiences to be experienced, expressed, and reflected upon in a way that will make them more meaningful, tolerable, and bearable (Allen, 2014). The prerequisite for talking about the trauma is a good relationship based on trust and patience.

What to do?

Take your time during the interview and show the necessary empathy to understand the child's situation.

Using the model, explain to the adolescent about re-enactment and explain that it is a normal reaction to a traumatic experience. Explain that we all need to understand what is happening both within us and around us, and that the brain tries to make sense of the incomprehensible via re-enactment. Also explain that re-enactment can be tempting, because it reminds us of the trauma. It is almost as if we become addicted to the experience and can only find peace through doing things reminding of the trauma.

Tips and tricks

Be interested and examine the child's own experiences and reason/motivation for re-enacting. The most important thing is that the child feels your sincere interest and desire to understand. Pay special attention to the child's thoughts and feelings. Examine possible experiences by saying: "Some people who have experienced something unpleasant may find themselves in situations that are reminiscent of what they have experienced before. It may be that you do something that you wish you had not done but find yourself in that same situation again and again. Is that something that you recognise?

Example

A girl living in an institution has been arguing with one of the other adolescents. The girl comes from a home where she was beaten by her father. When a teacher tries to come between the two, the girl sees red and strikes the teacher again and again. The teacher experiences the girl being out of reach/unable to contact/changing and not until afterwards does the girl realise what she has done and feels terrible.

Note: The exercise was prepared in cooperation with psychologist Line Sangild Thimmer and was inspired by Allen, Fonagy, and Bateman, 2010, and Hagelquist, 2012.

MODEL **RE-ENACTMENT**

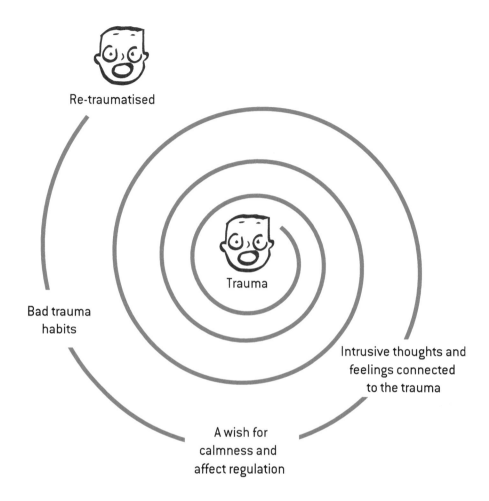

Re-traumatised

Trauma

Bad trauma
habits

Intrusive thoughts and
feelings connected
to the trauma

A wish for
calmness and
affect regulation

What can remind you of some of the terrible things that you have experienced? Can
you recognise feeling stressed and wishing to break free?

_____

_____

_____

_____

_____

_____

What situations can cause you to relive the experience?

_____

_____

_____

_____

_____

_____

How do you react in these situations?

_____

_____

_____

_____

_____

_____

How do you feel afterwards?

_____

_____

_____

_____

_____

_____

Trauma focus – ghosts in the nursery

Ghosts are pictures of negative events from childhood: ghosts haunt us and colour our interactions with those we love. If ghosts are let go and laid to rest, they can no longer haunt the living.

What to do?

Write about or draw your ghosts. One example is being told that everything is dangerous, so you are always afraid of new things. Another example is that you have been teased, so you are always sure that you are doing something wrong.

Tips and tricks

People protect themselves and cannot revisit their ghosts if they are not ready. Do not push if the child or adolescent does not seem ready.

> ### Example
> A boy talks about how he repeatedly found his mother after she attempted suicide, and how when he was small he had to call the ambulance over and over again and then watch her being carried away. He draws a large pill bottle inside the ghost.

Trauma focus – overcoming trauma

The treatment of trauma through mentalization partially involves capturing ghosts and making sure they are safely buried. Remember to say that it is quite common for ghosts to reappear during new crises, and there are often some ghosts that are not quite ready to be buried.

What to do?
When it seems meaningful to the treatment complete the model so that the child or adolescent can engage in an act that symbolises that the ghost is safely laid to rest.

Tips and tricks
The exercise is done following the ghost and angels exercises.

> **Example**
> A mother's son was very ill and she almost lost him when he was a baby. The boy is now healthy but the mother is always very concerned about him, and that has perhaps contributed to her son developing a phobia about school and being afraid to leave his mother. The exercise helps the mother understand what it takes to bury the ghost.

MODEL OVERCOMING TRAUMA

What traumas have you faced in your life?

_____

Can you see examples in your life today where they still affect you?

_____

_____

Are there examples where you see yourself acting in ways that would be reasonable in a traumatic situation, but not today?

_____

_____

Is there a way we can symbolically bury these ghosts?

_____

_____

Visualise that the ghosts have been laid to rest – for example, by saving this drawing and letting it be part of your story.

An example of this might be a visit to your childhood home to say goodbye to the ghosts.

Obtaining skills – emotions – what is inside your body

Emotions are grounded in the body. You can say that a child has emotions from birth but is not aware of them and cannot put them into inner boxes just yet. A child can feel the state that matches the emotion *anger*, but cannot not put it in the box that corresponds with *anger* and know, "What I am feeling is anger." He also cannot articulate the feeling, "I'm angry."

Human beings are predisposed to seek out interactions where their emotions can be mirrored. These interactions are the basis for a child to learn to detect his feelings, categorise them, and then be able to express them (Fonagy, Gergely, Jurist, & Target, 2007). If a child has not learned to register his emotions via typical evolutionary interactions, he must be taught how to become attentive to and register them.

What to do?

To assist a child in learning how to register his emotions, have him draw them into the illustration of the body on the following page. Tell the child: "We feel sensations and emotions in our body. Where in your body do you feel the different emotions: joy, sadness, fear, anger? Draw where you feel the different emotions in your body. Choose a colour that suits every emotion. Draw and explain the emotions."

Tips and tricks

The child can determine in advance what colour to assign to each emotion and create a colour chart beside the figure. In a group context, let children draw each other's silhouettes by tracing each other while they lie on the floor. Then chart the emotions of the body in each drawing.

Example

An eleven-year-old girl who has lived with sexual assault creates a representation of her body with her psychologist. She can only describe one emotion, anger, and chooses the colour black to represent it. She covers the drawing in black. When she has finished colouring, she is quiet and sad and talks about the emptiness she experiences. Two years later, she creates a new figure using several colours – anger is still part of the picture, but there is also sadness and joy. The new drawing is placed in her folder with the "black" image she made when she was younger. The psychiatrist and the girl both welcome the gains she has shown in her emotional life.

Obtaining skills – emotions – the compass of emotions

In mentalization-based teaching it is central to help the child register, categorise, and verbalise his emotional states. The emotional compass can be used to illustrate the importance of knowing one's own emotions.

What to do?

The compass of emotions can be used as a concrete starting point for a conversation with a child about emotions. Everyone has emotions. Do you know joy? When do you experience joy? Do you know anger? When do you get angry? What helps you when you are angry? How can someone tell when you are angry? What can adults do to help you when you are angry? What emotions do you know best?

Tips and tricks

Fill in the model and write or draw a story for every emotion.

> **Example**
> A fourteen-year-old boy thinks the exercise is ridiculous. "I have no emotions," he says. His teacher offers up examples for each emotion and the boy begins to tell some stories.

MODEL **THE COMPASS OF EMOTIONS**

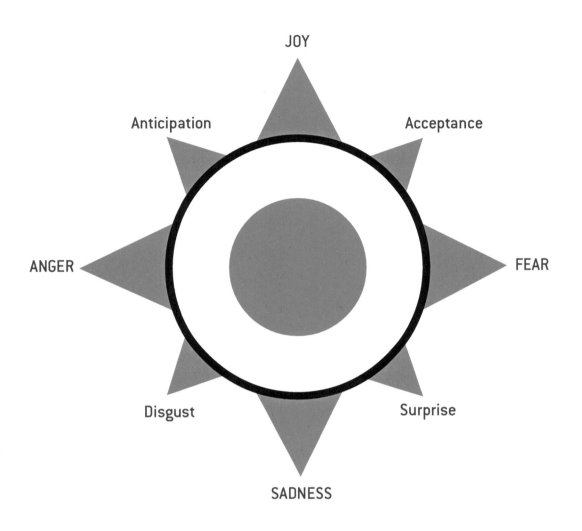

Obtaining skills – emotions – talking about emotions/a game with basic emotions

It is important to learn to express emotions – every emotion – not only joy. To motivate a child to verbalise his emotions it is necessary to understand the importance of emotions and to create an environment that focuses on emotions. As the Fonagy group say: "Emotionally modulated conversations are the royal road to mentalizing" (Allen, Fonagy, & Bateman, 2010, p. 131). They emphasise the point by adding: "We actually can not overemphasise the importance of allowing emotional expression" (p. 92).

During normal evolutionary interactions, children learn to register, categorise, and articulate emotions. When an adult recognises an emotion in a child, she reflects the emotion and puts it into words. With a slightly older child, the adult can articulate the emotion that the adult herself would experience in a given situation: "It makes me sad when someone takes my things," or "When I was young, one of my friends kissed my girlfriend and I was jealous and angry." It is important to create an environment where the child feels safe talking about emotions. Expressing emotions starts with a sense of safety with a caregiver. It can be both impractical and inappropriate to tell everything about your emotional states.

What to do?

There are a number of suggestions on how to encourage someone to talk about emotions. The key is to do it in a way that a child finds fun or meaningful. The following page offers a few suggestions – there is always room for more!

Tips and tricks

Certain statements should not be used when supporting a child in articulating his emotions: "What you really feel is …", "I think what you're really telling me is …", "I think that your expectations in this situation are too high …", or "You can probably see that this is your own fault …". Such statements will not help a child learn to register, categorise, and articulate his own emotional states.

Example

A sixteen-year-old boy visits a psychologist because he is not feeling well and he wonders how he can feel better when the world is so evil that children are exposed to violence and abuse. It turns out that the boy is not in touch with his own anger and anxiety. He is a talented artist and he draws pictures expressing anger and anxiety. He also begins to look for those emotions in music and later from peers who are better able to express their anger and anxiety in a constructive way.

MODEL WAYS OF TALKING ABOUT EMOTIONS

- Play a game of charades that display basic emotions. Write the emotions that the child understands on small pieces of paper. The child selects one and acts it out.

- Take photographs of different emotions as expressed by the child and his family.

- Read aloud from books with themes dealing with the child's experiences.

- Watch movies and television programmes that focus on people expressing emotions.

- Have the child draw himself expressing basic emotions.

- Keep a diary.

- Tell stories about other children or adolescents who have been in similar situations and that reflect the emotions that your child may be feeling (Andersen & Holter, 1997; Egelund et al., 1998).

- Help the child find music that represents his different emotions.

- Look in magazines to find photos of people expressing different basic emotions.

MODEL PLAY WITH BASIC EMOTIONS

Cut out the pictures and allow the child or adolescent to choose a feeling for the child to describe.

ANTICIPATION

JOY

ACCEPTANCE

ANGER

DISGUST

FEAR

SADNESS

SURPRISE

Obtaining skills – emotions – crisis plan

Mentalization-based teaching works with emotion regulation through the composition of crisis plans. A crisis plan is always individual and made in collaboration with the child. It should be as concrete as possible and contain a way to make contact with adults who can help. A crisis plan is key as it provides opportunities for support with self-regulation and help when emotions are too intense and difficult to regulate. A crisis plan is a way of creating a common focus for working on regulating emotions. Developing a crisis plan is a task of mentalizing itself.

Since the work of developing a crisis plan uses emotions as the basis for action, there is no automatic assumption that specific emotions lead to specific actions, and the child experiences something new: that situations do not have to end with struggles and violence.

What to do?

Develop, together with the child or adolescent, a crisis plan relating to a particular destructive or self-destructive behaviour. If possible, use the model on the following page. The adult must ask probing questions and be very specific. It is also important to remember that outlining a crisis plan is also mentalization training. Any crisis plan must be continuously evaluated and adapted based on new information.

Tips and tricks

The crisis plan can be printed on a laminated card that can be carried in a pocket (one for a young child could have a picture of the child's favourite animal on the back). The card must contain the crisis plan and include very specific instructions as to what to do when emotional intensity is running high.

Example

A fifteen-year-old girl cuts her arm when she feels abandoned. A crisis plan is prepared together with her teacher, instructing the girl as to what she should do when she feels the desire to cut herself. The girl cuts herself again after the plan is created and is found out. New ideas are developed as to what she can do when she feels the desire to cut herself.

MODEL CRISIS PLAN

In which situations is there a particular risk that things will go wrong?

_____

_____

Which emotions are especially difficult for you (anger, sadness, anxiety, feeling left behind)?

_____

_____

Do you have previous experience with doing something different in a situation so that you avoided the behaviour that the crisis plan is concerned with?

_____

_____

What can you do in the future rather than engaging in the behaviour that the crisis plan is concerned with?

_____

_____

Has anything that you have done before helped?

_____

_____

What can you think of that might help you when you are just about to do what the crisis plan is about ?

_____

_____

_____

Have those thoughts helped you before?

_____

_____

_____

How do you control your emotions in other situations? What do you usually do when you are angry or upset?

_____

_____

_____

Who can you contact or ask for help when you are about to engage in the behaviour this crisis plan is about?

_____

_____

_____

What will I see in you, when you are about to engage in the behaviour? What can I do to help you?

_____

_____

_____

Are there others who need to know how they can see that it is about to go wrong?

_____

_____

_____

Where will you keep the crisis plan so that you use it?

_____

_____

_____

Obtaining skills – emotions – sadness volume control button

Emotions should not only be registered, categorized, and articulated. They also need to be regulated. To be successful at regulating emotions, it is important that the child receives help to learn how to increase and decrease his personal volume button.

It is important that the child is allowed to practise. It's a bit like learning to drive a car on slippery roads and practising in wild and difficult situations. It can look quite hopeless at first, but by training and being allowed to make mistakes, you finally get it right down to the smallest details.

The child will need the opportunity to practise and learn how to be really upset. He should experience that it is possible to control emotions – first when working with an adult and ultimately alone.

As his abilities to increase and decrease the volume button on his own emotions grow, the adjustment should shift from being controlled by someone on the outside – the adult with the volume control – to the child as he grows up, in order for the child to be capable at regulating his own emotions.

What to do?

Talk about the "emotional volume control". Show the child the model and help him fill it out. Talk to the child about the need to be able to turn the volume button up and down. Even adults sometimes need someone to help them change the volume, but it's great to be able to do it on your own and to know who and how others can help you, when it gets too difficult.

Tips and tricks

If a child can not recall situations of various emotional intensity, be prepared with stories from your own life or other children you have met.

Example

An eight-year-old boy lost his mother in a car accident. There had only been the two of them in their home, and he is sure that if he allows himself to cry, he will never stop. He and his social worker at the orphanage are working on a model intended to teach him to control his emotions in the same way he controls the music on his smartphone. He has to turn it up and down to find the place where it sounds the best. The speaker is constructed so that it can cope with being turned completely up or down. They slowly begin to talk about loss and missing another person.

MODEL SADNESS VOLUME CONTROL BUTTON

Name three examples where you have felt sadness as it compares to the different spots on the volume control:

An example of feeling a little sad:

_____

An example of feeling sad:

_____

An example of feeling very sad:

_____

Can you turn the volume down yourself?

_____

How?

_____

What can others do to help you turn the volume down?

_____

EXERCISES

Obtaining skills – emotions – joy volume control button

Emotions should not only be registered, categorized, and articulated. They also need to be controlled. To be good at controlling emotions, it is important that a child learns how to increase and decrease the volume button.

It is important that the child is allowed to practise. It's a bit like learning to drive a car on slippery roads and practising in wild and difficult situations. It can look quite hopeless at first, but by training and being allowed to make mistakes, you finally get it right down to the fine details.

The child will need the opportunity to practise and learn how to be very happy. He should experience that it is possible to control emotions – first when working with an adult and ultimately alone.

As his abilities to increase and decrease the volume button on his own emotions grow, the adjustment should shift from being controlled by someone on the outside – the adult with the volume control – to the child.

What to do?

Talk about the "emotional volume control". Show the child the model and help him fill it out. Talk to the child about the need to be able to change the volume. Even adults sometimes need someone to help them change the volume, but it's great to be able to do it on your own.

Tips and tricks

If a child can not recall situations of different emotional intensity, be prepared with stories from your own life or other children you have met.

Example
A thirteen-year-old girl attending a special class for children with social and emotional difficulties talks with her teacher. She has trouble when she and her girlfriends get laughing fits during class. She cannot stop, and it often ends with her being so overly excited that she does something foolish: she might pull the hair of one of the girls not in on the fun or possibly throw things. Together they work within the model and talk about how she can turn down the volume when she feels too happy.

MODEL **JOY VOLUME CONTROL BUTTON**

Name three examples where you have felt happiness as it compares to the different spots on the volume control:

An example of feeling a little happy:

_____

An example of feeling happy:

_____

An example of feeling very happy:

_____

Can you turn the volume down yourself?

_____

How?

_____

What can others do to help you turn the volume down?

_____

Obtaining skills – emotions – anger volume control button

Emotions should not only be registered, categorised, and articulated. They also need to be controlled. To be good at controlling emotions, it is important that a child learns how to increase and decrease the volume button.

It is important that the child is allowed to practise. It's a bit like learning to drive a car on slippery roads and practising in wild and difficult situations. It can look quite hopeless at first, but by training and being allowed to make mistakes, you finally get it right down to the smallest details.

The child will need the opportunity to practise and learn how to be very angry. He should experience that it is possible to control emotions – first when working with an adult and ultimately alone.

As his abilities to increase and decrease the volume button on his own emotions grow, the adjustment should shift from being controlled by someone on the outside – the adult with the volume control – to the child.

What to do?

Talk about the "emotional volume control". Show the child the model and help him fill it out. Talk to the child about the need to be able to change the volume. Even adults sometimes need someone to help them change the volume, but it's great to be able to do it on your own.

Tips and tricks

If a child can not recall situations of different emotional intensity, be prepared with stories from your own life or other children you have met.

Example

A nine-year-old boy has difficulty controlling his temper. He loves football, but whenever he is tackled roughly, he becomes so angry that he hits and kicks. He does not even think that he has a volume button. "When I get angry, everything turns black," he says. He fills out the model, and after many crisis plans he becomes better at controlling his anger volume control.

MODEL **ANGER VOLUME CONTROL BUTTON**

Name three examples where you have felt anger as it compares to the different spots on the volume control:

An example of feeling a little angry:

_____

An example of feeling angry:

_____

An example of feeling very angry:

_____

Can you turn the volume down yourself?

_____

How?

_____

What can others do to help you turn the volume down?

_____

Obtaining skills – emotions – fear volume control button

Emotions should not only be recorded, categorised, and articulated. They also need to be controlled. To be good at controlling emotions, it is important that a child learns how to increase and decrease the volume button.

It is important that the child is allowed to practise. It's a bit like learning to drive a car on slippery roads and practising in wild and difficult situations. It can look quite hopeless at first, but by training and being allowed to make mistakes, you finally get it right down to the smallest details.

The child will need the opportunity to practise and learn how to be afraid. He should experience that it is possible to control emotions – first when working with an adult and ultimately alone.

As his abilities to increase and decrease the volume button on his own emotions grow, the adjustment should shift from being controlled by someone on the outside – the adult with the volume control – to the child.

What to do?

Talk about the "emotional volume control". Show the child the model and help him fill it out. Talk to the child about the need to be able to change the volume. Even adults sometimes need someone to help them change the volume, but it's great to be able to do it on your own.

Tips and tricks

If a child can not recall situations of different emotional intensity, be prepared with stories from your own life or other children you have met.

Example

A six-year-old boy starts to go to a psychologist due to fear. He has been repeatedly hospitalised due to heart disease. During the initial conversation, it becomes apparent that his parents become very frightened whenever the boy becomes afraid. Because the bodily reactions of fear are similar to the symptoms of heart problems and because the parents have been afraid of losing their son, the parents struggle to endure and regulate their anxiety. The psychologist uses the emotional compass to talk about the importance of feeling fear and applies the model to teach the boy that fear can be experienced in different ways, and that you can learn to turn the feelings up and down.

MODEL FEAR VOLUME CONTROL BUTTON

Name three examples where you have felt fear as it compares to the different spots on the volume control:

An example of being a little afraid:

_____

An example of being afraid:

_____

An example of feeling very afraid:

_____

Can you turn the volume down yourself?

_____

How?

_____

What can others do to help you turn the volume down?

_____

EXERCISES

Obtaining skills – emotions – symptoms of anxiety

Anxiety symptoms are very strong because fear can be important in relation to taking care of ourselves and surviving. We know, for example, that fear in the face of dangerous tigers leads to bodily reactions that make one act quickly.

Learning to regulate anxiety comes from the outside in. When anxiety is not under control, the child may experience anxiety attacks. It is important to identify the physical symptoms of anxiety as what they are and not an indication that something fatal is wrong with the body. It should, of course, be ascertained that the symptoms are not the result of a disease.

What to do?

Explain to the child about the importance of anxiety as an intense signal to the body and that it can be a good thing to experience it in everyday situations. The body is telling you there is something wrong and that something needs to be done. The therapist reads the list and asks the child which symptoms he recognises.

Tips and tricks

When working with anxiety, it is very important that the therapist is calm and signals that anxiety is something you can learn to regulate. In this way, the therapist is seen as part of the regulatory process.

Example

A boy comes to a psychologist because he has had several violent anxiety attacks in social situations. The psychologist shows him the list and says, "It sounds as if fear is what we need to get a handle on." The boy is very surprised and says again and again: "I have all of these strange symptoms. Is it just fear? I thought it was something that could kill me!"

MODEL SYMPTOMS OF ANXIETY

When one is very frightened, the body can send signals that something very dangerous has happened. All these symptoms are related to fear and are not dangerous in themselves.

Things that happen in the body when you are afraid:
- Rapid heartbeat

- Cold sweat

- Nausea

- Tremors

- Nervousness

- Dry mouth

- Shortness of breath/breathing problems

- Fear of dying

- Fear of doing something insane

- Feeling of choking

- Dizziness

- Feeling being disconnected from reality

- Numbness/tingling in hands, lips, and skin

- Stomach ache

Obtaining skills – emotions – anxiety hierarchy

Most trauma treatment programmes have overcoming avoidance as a separate treatment element. Avoidance may occur at a number of levels: by avoiding emotions, by avoiding dealing with or talking about an event or through behaviour that avoids situations similar to the incident (APA, 1994).

Part of the work in avoidance is to distinguish between good and bad avoidance. The treatment works to reduce the anxiety and assure the child that the anxiety can be regulated and he can learn how to reduce anxiety.

However, it is important to work to overcome avoidance in a way so that the child feels secure and that the work will not cause him to be re-traumatised (Peterson, Prout, & Schwartz, 1991; Schiraldi, 2000).

What to do?

Design a fear hierarchy with the child in relation to something specific that he is very afraid of. Ask the child what he is afraid of. Start with the easiest task at the bottom of the hierarchy. The goals and tasks should be reachable, so that the child experiences a sense of success in overcoming fear. The professional can be present when the child performs the tasks. The agreement should support and reward the child for every task.

On the next page is an example of an anxiety hierarchy for a child who has a phobia about going to school. The following page includes a chart that can be filled out with an anxiety hierarchy.

Tips and tricks

Those working with children can work to make the anxiety hierarchy even more festive by drawing a flag when the child achieves the next level, and by writing letters to the child about the next step. It can also be a good idea to give the thing the child is afraid of a name: the Scary Monster, the School Phobia Troll, the Puke Beast.

Example

Jack has developed a phobia about school, and he has not been to school for half a year. An anxiety hierarchy is developed together with Jack's psychologist and an educator who is recruited to help Jack come back to school.

MODEL JACK'S ANXIETY HIERARCHY

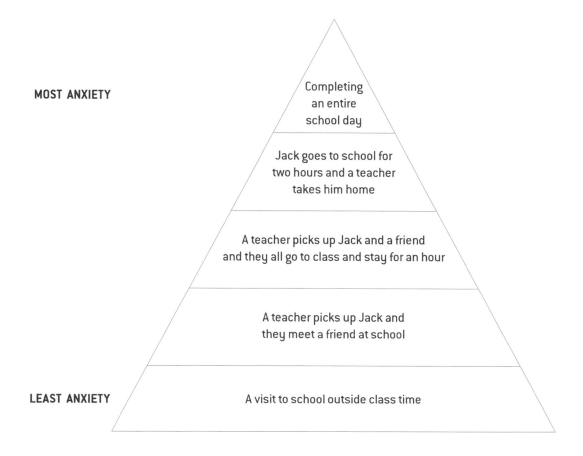

MOST ANXIETY

Completing
an entire
school day

Jack goes to school for
two hours and a teacher
takes him home

A teacher picks up Jack and a friend
and they all go to class and stay for an hour

A teacher picks up Jack and
they meet a friend at school

LEAST ANXIETY

A visit to school outside class time

MODEL **ANXIETY HIERARCHY**

MOST ANXIETY

LEAST ANXIETY

Obtaining skills – behaviour – strategies for regulating behaviour

Often behaviour is the first skill you are most tempted to work with, but if inappropriate behaviour is due to a lack of skills in another area, correcting the behaviour will not be possible until other skills are developed. For example, self-destructive behaviour can rarely be remedied without simultaneously working with an adolescent's ability to control his emotions. However, behaviour must not be ignored so that inappropriate behaviour is allowed to develop (Hagelquist, 2012; Webster-Stratton, 2009).

What to do?

The list on the next page provides suggestions for behavioural strategies and must be used in a mentalizing manner.

Tips and tricks

The least intrusive strategies are mentioned first. More of these should be used than those at the bottom. Always work within the intervention spectrum in mind (see p. 71).

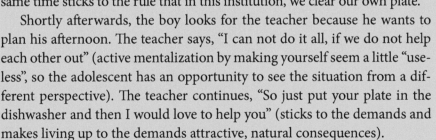

Example

A fourteen-year-old boy has just moved in to a residential institution. He is very confrontational with the staff. At one point after a meal he is asked to put his plate into the dishwasher. His teacher has suggested three strategies: give one task at a time, ask positively, and express confidence. The boy refuses and leaves the room to play on his computer. The teacher lets him go (avoid power struggles, ignore inappropriate behaviour), but makes an inclusive funny comment (humour) that doesn't humiliate the boy and at the same time sticks to the rule that in this institution, we clear our own plate.

Shortly afterwards, the boy looks for the teacher because he wants to plan his afternoon. The teacher says, "I can not do it all, if we do not help each other out" (active mentalization by making yourself seem a little "useless", so the adolescent has an opportunity to see the situation from a different perspective). The teacher continues, "So just put your plate in the dishwasher and then I would love to help you" (sticks to the demands and makes living up to the demands attractive, natural consequences).

The boy goes out and puts his plate in the dishwasher, and the teacher praises him (praise). Throughout the interaction, the teacher focuses on recognition and reflection. The teacher is able to create a sense of peace and reflection in herself so that the situation does not escalate.

MODEL STRATEGIES FOR REGULATING CONDUCT

- Praise and be encouraging concerning the desired behaviour

- Give specific praise

- Praise in the presence of others

- Express confidence

- Give one task at a time

- Be positive when addressing the child with demands

- Acknowledge the difficulty about demands

- Offer choices when possible

- Use distraction

- Use humour

- Be consistent about demands in a mentalizing way/manner

- Use active mentalization – draw attention to your own mental states, if necessary by making yourself seem "useless"

- Avoid power struggles

- Ignore inappropriate behaviour – disconnect – and return attention to the adolescent when he shows the desired behaviour

- Create incentives to meet requirements

- Be consistent, but not through punitive behaviour

Obtaining skills – behaviour – pros and cons

Part of changing behaviour is grounded in motivation. Work on motivation consists, among other things, in realising the benefits and drawbacks of a particular behaviour. Talking about the advantages and disadvantages bring the mental states behind the behaviour into play. The motivation for change comes from within and can not be imposed from outside, no matter how much you may want to try. Unfortunately, coercion usually only creates further resistance. Motivation fluctuates over time, so the model may need to be used several times. Change happens best when supported by a relationship. The model may be a way for the caregiver and the child to find direction within the chaos together. Through the model, the child can find his own words to explain the advantages and disadvantages. This makes it possible to understand the behaviour in a more reflective manner.

What to do?
Talk to the child or adolescent about the pros and cons of a particular behaviour. It can be large or small: going to school, having contact with a father who has let them down, alcohol or drug abuse, cutting themselves, prostitution, leaving a violent boyfriend, and trying something new.

On the left side of the scales, write down the positive reasons/benefits. On the right side of the scales, write down all of the negative reasons/disadvantages.

Tips and tricks
It is fundamental during the exercise to maintain an Open mind. It can be hard not to interject and continue rather to be curious and empathetic when you have intense feelings and want to prevent the child from engaging in destructive behaviour.

Example
A thirteen-year-old girl repeatedly runs away from her residential institution to engage in prostitution. Many things are attempted to prevent this very destructive behaviour. But the girl continues again and again to meet with adult men who abuse her. It is difficult for her psychologist to use the pros and cons chart without injecting his own presuppositions, but he manages. They talk about the advantages: money, a sense of control and comfort. More importantly – once the girl has been allowed to articulate the benefits, she must also articulate the consequences.

MODEL **PROS AND CONS**

PROS	CONS

Obtaining skills – behaviour – chain analysis

Chain analysis is used to analyse an event where mentalization has failed. The chain analysis is different from trigger analysis in that there need not be a specific trauma-trigger, but a process that evolved inappropriately and resulted in a mentalization failure. The model allows analysis of situations with emphasis both on vulnerability factors, events, thoughts, feelings, actions, and on consequences. The professional's emotions and behaviour and the consequences are also included in the analysis.

What to do?

Chain analysis is used to analyse a specific case scenario from both the child's and the adult's perspective. What were the reasons behind the specific behaviour/action? Which internal triggers (feelings, thoughts, etc.) and external (the behaviour of others, smells, sounds, etc.) triggered the behaviour? What consequences resulted in the child's and the professional's behaviour?

The chain analysis is reviewed along with the child or youth in order to sensitise their thoughts, feelings, etc. in connection with a specific behaviour so that the child can more easily understand the context of his thoughts and feelings about his behaviour and actions, and the consequences that the behaviour and actions have caused. Chain analysis is valuable to the staff as self-assessment and to sensitise the employee's thoughts and feelings, which can be useful in future conflicts/situations where chain analysis can help employees involved in those later conflicts maintain a mentalized setting.

Tips and tricks

Chain analysis can be done with the child or staff where different suggestions can be made about where the child may be vulnerable and what he may have thought and felt in a particular situation.

Example
A fourteen-year-old boy is on a trip with his residential institution. They must climb a hill, and in the middle of an otherwise pleasant walk, the boy hits a smaller boy very hard in the head. The teacher on the trip is frightened and grabs the boy. He shouts at the boy and pulls him back to the car. The following day, the boy and the teacher do a chain analysis together. It turns out that the younger boy has said that he would beat the fourteen year old's beloved dog to death. Based on this knowledge, they help each other complete a chain analysis.

Note: The model was developed in collaboration with psychologist Natasa Zoric.

MODEL CHAIN ANALYSIS 1 – CHILD/YOUTH

Vulnerability factors	Triggers	Thoughts	Emotions	Actions/ behaviour	Conse- quences

MODEL CHAIN ANALYSIS 2 – STAFF

Emotions	Actions/behaviour	Consequences

Obtaining skills – behaviour – reflect and repair

Following a breakdown in mentalization where the child or adolescent has experienced intense emotions and perhaps acted inappropriately, time should be taken to reflect on what happened. What are the feelings underlying the behaviour? Go back and see what happened just before the outburst, such as self-destructive behaviour when the child ran away or something similar. The child and teachers can use this opportunity to understand and make sense of the reasons for the child's behaviour. Repairing is in this way created within a mentalizing framework.

What to do?

A "reflect and repair" meeting should only be held after the emotional intensity level has fallen and everyone has re-established their mentalization abilities. Those involved should meet and discuss what happened. This can also be a way of finding out how to repair what happened. Try to get the adolescent to make suggestions about how things can be better (Rossouw, 2012). Sometimes that means examining reasonable consequences in relation to what happened. That could include making an apology or financial compensation. The child and teachers can use this opportunity to understand and make sense of the reasons for the child's behaviour.

Tips and tricks

A chain analysis completed with the child or adolescent could prove useful. Save the "reflect and repair" notes and look at them from time to time in order to learn from what seems to be particularly difficult.

Example

A girl becomes so furious that she smashes a window at her residential institution. At the "reflect and repair" meeting it is revealed that she had just been told that she can no longer call her mother without a teacher present, and then only once a week. The reason was that her mother could not stand/put up with the girl's many calls. When a teacher asks the girl if she would leave the common room because she needs to have a serious conversation with someone else, the girl perceives it as everyone hating her and wanting to be rid of her.

At the "reflect and repair" meeting, the girl understands the teacher's intention. A plan is made for the girl to call her insurance company to see if they will cover the cost of the window. Otherwise, she is ready to pay for it out of her allowance.

MODEL REFLECT AND REPAIR

How would you describe what happened? Elaborate on what you thought and felt:

_____

_____

_____

_____

_____

_____

How do you think others experienced what happened?

_____

_____

_____

_____

_____

_____

What can you do to repair what happened? (Apologise, pay for damages, etc.)

_____

_____

_____

_____

_____

_____

Obtaining skills – behaviour – mentalized boundary setting

Collaborative problem solving (in three stages) is a process in which cooperation is created between the adolescent and the adult in relation to handling challenging behavior. Early cooperation between the adolescent and the adult in the relationship can be developed in order to help handle challenging behaviour. The model was created by Ross Greene and is developed in more detail here as it relates to mentalization-based boundary setting (Greene, 2009). The purpose of the model is to solve problems in a sustainable manner, teaching adolescents skills that they lack and creating better conditions for interaction.

What to do?
Use the model in relation to a specific recurring behaviour that creates problems for the adolescent and/or the adults.

Tips and tricks
Remember that all three steps are essential, and that none of them can be omitted. Even if the child has difficulty communicating his feelings, thoughts, reasons, and needs, it is important not to give up – it can sometimes be helpful to ask the child to specify the who, what, where of the problem.

Educated guesses and testing hypotheses may be necessary if the child has a hard time getting started on his own.

It can be problematic if cooperative problem solving begins with the professional having a predetermined solution in mind, or if the terms "right" and "wrong" come into play.

Example
Step 1: Empathy
Use the Open stance to create the best possible understanding of the child's/adolescent's anxiety and/or the needs of the situation. Mirror and appreciate emotions, thoughts, and needs and help to put into words.

Step 2: Define the problem
The adult takes into account her concerns or needs while working towards finding a common solution to the individual issues of the two parties involved. There can only be a solution when there are two clearly defined issues on the table.

Step 3: Invitation
The adolescent is invited to try to solve the problem through joint brainstorming sessions and cooperation.

Note: The exercise was developed in collaboration with psychologist Gro Katborg.

MODEL **MENTALIZED BOUNDARY SETTING**

Step 1: Empathy – what do you think the problem is about?

_____

_____

_____

_____

_____

_____

Step 2: Define the problem – my concerns are ...

_____

_____

_____

_____

_____

_____

Step 3: Invitation – how can we find a joint solution?

_____

_____

_____

_____

_____

_____

Obtaining skills – attention/cognition

According to Kolk (2005a), there are countless studies that suggest that neglected and traumatised children have severe attention problems. The explanation is that when the child experiences trauma from his primary caregivers, the child's attention is focused on the caregiver rather than examining his external world. The ability to pay attention requires adults who support the child constantly expanding his attention span. If the child lives in an environment where development is not supported, this skill will not have the right circumstances to develop.

There are also genetic correlations that play a part in this development.

What to do?

When a child has difficulty paying attention, he will need help rehabilitating the ability. This is accomplished by the child once again experiencing success in relation to mastering the ability to pay attention. The model is used in the child's daily life, and the exercises are adapted to the stages the child has reached in both his developmental and chronological ages.

Tips and tricks

It is a constant question as to why children or adolescents who have attention disorders can focus on computer games for extended periods of time. Whether the games help to develop attention is outside the scope of this guide to define, but saying to the child or adolescent – "You focus very well when playing games, how can we use that to help with other situations in your life?" – helps articulate the child's resources and forces and that is always a good point for attention training.

Example

A fifteen-year-old boy bakes a cake with his favourite teacher. The teacher structures the entire process so that the boy is constantly experiencing success, and so the individual challenges during the baking process have a beginning and an end. The teacher says: "Now we put in the egg and stir. That was super, and now we …" The teacher guides the boy the whole time: "Now you are getting a little restless, but you're almost done …" The boy ends up finishing the cake and they enjoy it with the other adolescents at the facility.

MODEL ATTENTION/COGNITION

- Be the facilitator of activities with clear starting and ending points.

- Activities should have a fixed time frame (use an egg timer or something similar).

- The adult trains the adolescent's attention abilities by pointing, showing, conversation, and storytelling. As some adolescents are often very self-absorbed, a secondary benefit of this approach is that the adolescent trains his social skills by engaging in joint attention.

- Identify and help the child/adolescent to understand the internal and external causes of attention disruption, in order to teach the child to control them, so that they don't control the child:

  - Outer: disorder, noise (from phones, music, chatter), computers, and mobile phones

  - Internal: hunger, fatigue, boredom, resentment, lack of motivation/interest, performance anxiety, lack of perspective, daydreams, concerns

- Pay attention to the condition of the body's own states, emotions, and thoughts – take a very concrete approach: "What do you feel in your body right now?", "What are you thinking?" – or, more advanced: "What are you feeling right now?"

- Do listening and repeating exercises

- Develop a strategy for how a seemingly daunting task can be accomplished through planning and dividing it into smaller parts

- Help creating structure, clarity, overview, predictability

- Help creating regular routines

- Give short and precise instructions

- Avoiding stressful situations when learning

- Give the proper amount of support (too little aid may cause the adolescent to become exasperated – too much can lead to learned helplessness).

Obtaining skills – physical – registering body sensations

Children learn to detect physical phenomena via ordinary development enhancing interactions with their caregivers. When older children have not learned these skills, they can be at a very early level developmentally in relation to physical regulation. However, they need to be treated based on their chronological age. Here are some ideas on how to frame an older child's level of development in a sufficiently challenging way. The best way to do it is through play. Lev Vygotsky emphasised that "… during play, the child is always older than his actual age and is always more advanced than his daily behaviour; during play, it is as if the child is a head taller than himself" (Fonagy, Gergely, Jurist, & Target, 2007, p. 248).

What to do?

The model contains ideas on how to teach children to detect bodily sensations, but there are many other ways to support children in becoming better able to detect their physical conditions. One thing that all the ideas have in common is that they include as much fun and play as possible.

Tips and tricks

You can also experiment with regulating physical conditions by playing games that involve turning intensity up and down. It may be old-fashioned children's games like "Musical Chairs", "Dodgeball", or "Tag".

Example

A twelve-year-old boy has a very poor sense of his own body. He wears heavy sweaters in the summer, and goes shoeless in the snow during winter without noticing. He is the type who constantly runs into things. His foster mother says, "He can't poke a stick into a piece of shit without ruining both of them." The family is working on many levels to support the boy becoming better able to detect and categorise his physical condition.

MODEL REGISTERING BODY SENSATIONS

- Provide massage, for example, foot massage

- Go into the sauna

- Encourage games where the focus is turning the volume control up and down

- Experiment feeling the difference between hot and cold water

- Draw on the back of the child — the child must guess what you are drawing

- Make a "sandwich" by rolling the child inside a mattress pad and push on it from the outside

- Stack your and the child's hands alternately

- Find birthmarks

- Pull gently on each of the child's fingers

- Experiment with tactile sensations of different types of materials: velvet, silk, leather

- Tickle with a feather

- Rub on some cream

- Go swimming

- Notice how your body feels. "Were you breathless?", "Your hands are freezing, do you feel cold?", "Try to feel whether you feel full. How can you tell that you are full?

Obtaining skills – self – what is happening inside your head?

The child benefits from learning that the things that go on inside his mind are meaningful. The model makes it clear that there are many different things going on in a person's mind. The model should be completed along with the child's parents, who, during the process, show the child that they are curious, open, and interested in the child's mind. The model can be used to develop greater interest in the many things going on inside the child's mind.

What to do?

Instruct the child to start by saying: "We all think and feel different things at different times. Some things take up more space than others." "Draw the various thoughts and emotions filling your head right now – give every thought and feeling a colour, and colour in the amount of space that every thought and emotion fills."

There are two drawings on the following pages that can be used for this.

Tips and tricks

It may be a good idea to draw or do something else while the child is drawing. It is important to create an atmosphere where the child is in the flow and enjoys drawing. It can be distracting if the caregiver and other family members disturb the child while he is drawing.

Example

A ten-year-old girl draws a trampoline and some candy and says, "My foster mother promised that I would get candy and that she would jump on a trampoline with me if I came here. I want to go home and eat candy. It's the only thing in my head." The model was an eye-opener for the foster mother, who was focused on the abuse the girl had suffered. It opened up a conversation about how the girl sometimes thought about the assault, but at other times she had the same thoughts and needs as an ordinary ten-year-old.

MODEL WHAT IS HAPPENING INSIDE YOUR HEAD?

Obtaining skills – self – the inside and outside of a box

One of mentalization's four dimensions is inside/outside. Being aware that there are differences in inner states and what can be seen on the outside is a way to train your mentalization abilities. At the same time, the exercise is "I-supportive" as the child finds photographs in magazines and draws pictures which helps clarify things for him.

What to do?

Buy cake boxes at the bakery – those that have not yet been assembled and still must be folded. Use the box for working with the concept of inside/outside.

Let the child draw or use material from magazines to represent his inner and outer selves. Teach the child that the outside is what others see: "How you appear from the outside." The inside of the box is what is inside you: "Your own thoughts, feelings, needs and goals."

Tips and tricks

For children who are not very familiar with expressing how they feel, the photos from the magazine are helpful as they can cut them out and glue them to the cake box.

Example

A thirteen-year-old girl makes a cake box with a smiley face and a cool girl on the outside. She paints the inside completely black and in one corner she sticks a picture of a little girl crying.

MODEL THE OUTSIDE OF A BOX

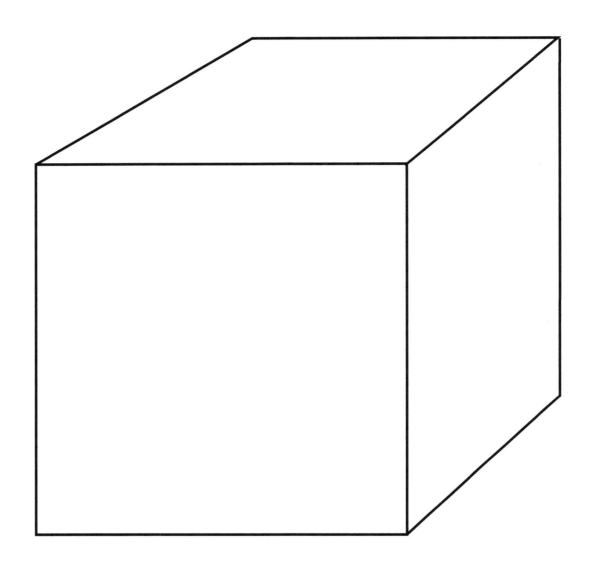

MODEL THE INSIDE OF A BOX

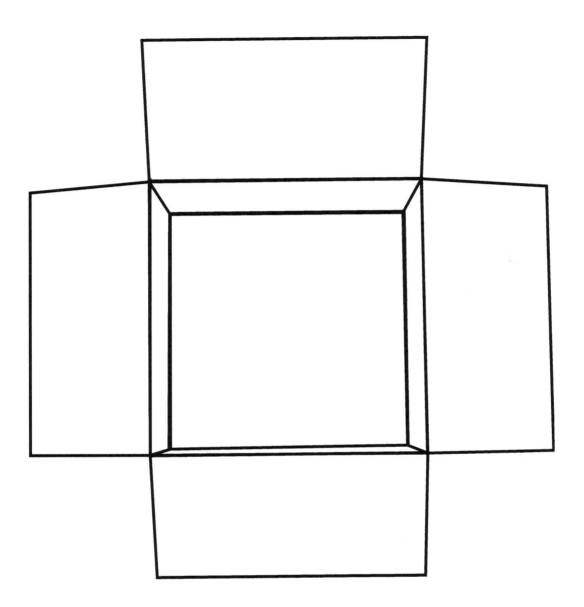

Obtaining skills – self – brain scan

"Brain scanning" is a way of working with the parents' understanding of a child's mental state. By talking about what happens inside a child's mind, parents can more closely examine the child's mental state. This externalisation makes it possible to reinforce the parents' curiosity for the child's mental states. The exercise is inspired by Eia Asen and used at the Anna Freud Centre in their mentalization-based family therapy.

What to do?

The therapist introduces the brain scan by playing a game. The therapist explains that they were lucky enough to get hold of a "brain scanner app". It is completely new and can be used to scan brains. The therapist takes his cell phone and takes a "picture" of the child's brain and says that he has now done a brain scan, but that he needs help filling it in to see if the scanner is working. The therapist then brings out the models. It is possible that only the child draws inside the brain scan picture, but the parents may also participate. This makes it possible to show parents that they can also reflect on the child's mental state.

Tips and tricks

When looking closely at behaviour that parents think is problematic, it is important to make the atmosphere fun and playful so that the child is willing to explore the mental states behind the behaviour.

Example

An eleven-year-old girl has many conflicts with her mother. The mother feels that she is doing everything she can to please the girl, but the girl is still always upset and angry with her. The last concrete example of this was a gymnastic exhibition that the girl wanted her mother to record on her iPhone. The girl draws a picture showing how much she had been looking forward to showing the video to her father, who was not present. She draws her face full of tears showing her sadness that she could not show the video. Through the "scan", she can now see that her mother was also angry with herself and upset that she failed to record the show.

Note: The exercise was developed by Eia Asen (Skårderud & Sommerfeldt, 2014) with inspiration from the Anna Freud Centre.

MODEL "BRAIN SCAN"

Name:

_____

Age:

_____

The parent's experience of the problem:

_____

The brain scan reveals that the child's reasons for the behaviour are:

_____

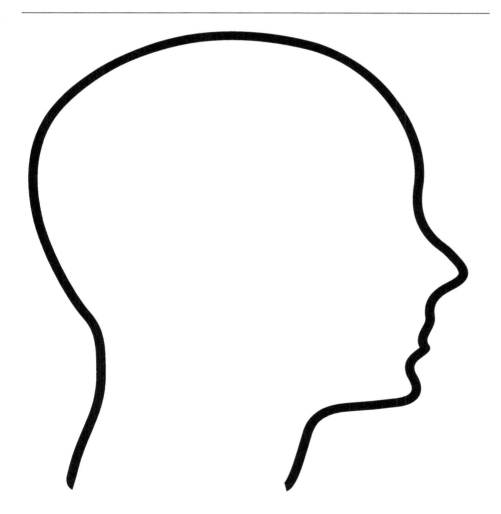

Obtaining skills – self – life stories

Speaking to an adolescent about his life can contribute to the adolescent's building a coherent life story and a feeling of being the same over time. Working with his life story can contribute to the integration and acceptance of his life. It is important to have an Open mind when working with life stories. Adults should be cautious and under no circumstances push if the adolescent chooses not to participate or will not talk about specific events. Adults can benefit from making sure to ask for both positive and negative experiences. Although there may be predominantly negative and unpleasant memories ("ghosts in the nursery"), it is also important to recall positive and pleasant experiences ("angels in the nursery"). This helps to create balance and nuance in the life story.

What to do?

If the adolescent agrees, the professional can work together with him and describe the adolescent's life in a lifeline as shown below. The line begins at conception or birth and ends in the present.

Tips and tricks

Include the births of siblings, moving days, illnesses, holidays, new beginnings like school starts, kindergarten, day care, significant adults, animals, and playmates. The first, best, worst, and most dangerous memories. You can make the timeline using flowers for good events and black leaves for negative events.

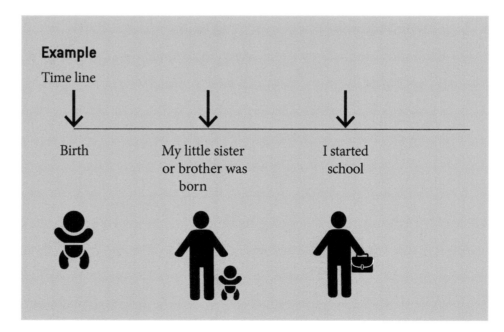

Example

Time line

| Birth | My little sister or brother was born | I started school |

MODEL **MY LIFE STORY**

My timeline

→ I was born

Obtaining skills – relationships – brain scan for parents and child

"The brain scan" can be used to work with the mental states of both children and adults in connection with a conflict in the family. By talking about the brain scan and letting the conversation about the conflict become a drawing exercise, the causes of the conflict are externalised and thereby become visible. It is no longer something that happened between "us", but something our brains do. This externalisation makes it possible to acknowledge the mental states each one experienced during the conflict. It is important to select a relatively new conflict, where emotions are still warm. Mentalization is best practised when challenged. One must be careful, however, not to choose conflicts that are too recent and where emotions are running too high. This creates the risk of starting a new conflict and suffering another mentalization failure.

What to do?

The therapist introduces the brain scan by launching the game. The therapist explains that they were lucky enough to get hold of a "brain scanner app". It is completely new and can be used to scan brains. The therapist takes his cell phone and takes a "picture" of the child's brain and says that he has now done a brain scan, but that he needs help filling it in to see if the scanner is working. The therapist then brings out the models. One is given to each family member and everyone sits quietly and writes and draws what they felt and thought and what they believed others felt and thought during the conflict.

Tips and tricks

Sometimes the models get filled in quickly, so it may be a good idea to have several ready. If the family enjoys the exercise, several models of various conflict situations can be made that will perhaps reveal patterns that appear in conflict situations.

Example

A father and his daughter talk about a conflict they had the day before. The father had eaten some of the girl's mints, and she was very upset. The girl said that during the disagreement her father had become a "screaming monster". They both make a "brain scan". The girl draws fine stick figures that show she understands that her father may have really wanted some mints. The father is surprised that his daughter seems to understand him, but is very sad that she sees him as "a monster".

Note: The exercise was developed by Eia Asen (Skårderud & Sommerfeldt, 2014) with inspiration from the Anna Freud Centre.

MODEL BRAIN SCAN FOR TWO

Brain scans dealing with conflicts in the family

MODEL BRAIN SCAN FAMILIES

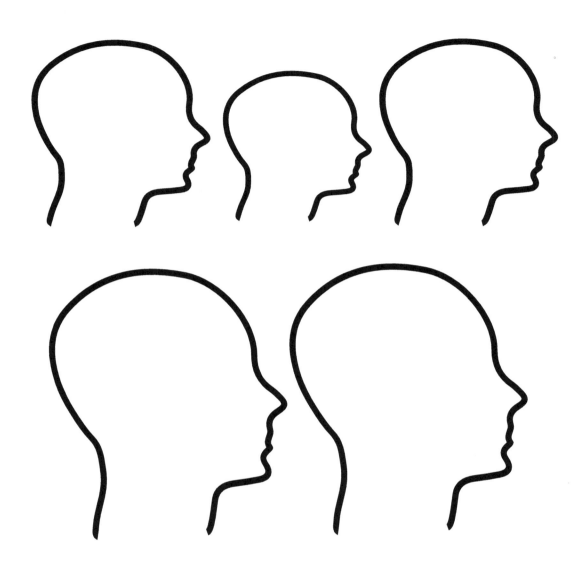

Obtaining skills – relations – family tree

Part of mentalization is seeing oneself in a developmental perspective. It can therefore be meaningful to develop a family tree at the beginning of treatment.

Children are attached to, addicted to, and a product of their parents. It is particularly important to understand the child within the context of the family that the child is experiencing.

What to do?

Design a family tree with the child. The adult asks about the members of the child's family. Draw it on a blank piece of paper as shown or use the next page. Ask about the child's relationship with individual family members: "How old are they?", "What do they do?", "Where do they live?", and "How are they getting along?" You can also ask about trauma, violence, alcohol, and abuse.

It is important to draw pictures of the positive relations the child has had – even if they are not part of the child's family.

Tips and tricks

If there are other significant people in the child's life, these should also be included.

> **Example**
> Two sisters who have been placed in care due to sexual abuse by their parents draw a family tree. They use different colours to show individual family members who have been abused, who have violated others, who have been violent, and who have been abusive. Slowly, the drawing begins to fill up with colour as the girls work together at understanding their family.

MODEL **FAMILY TREE**

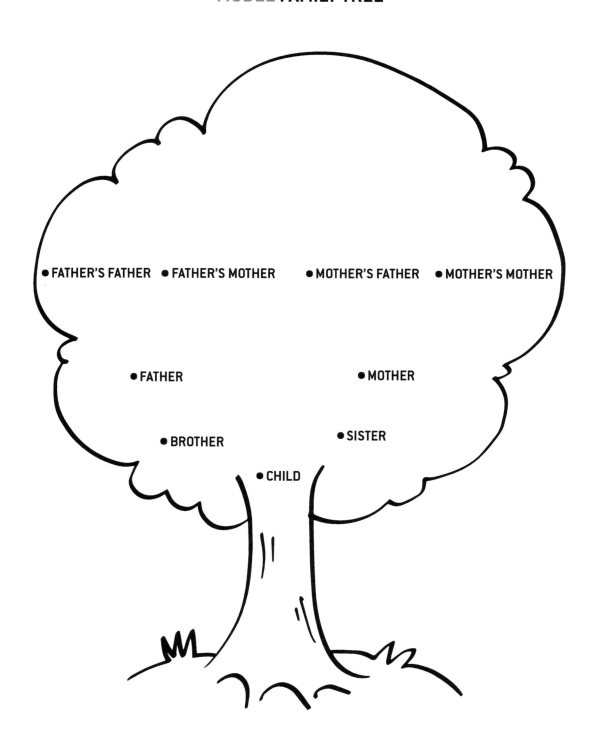

Obtaining skills – relationships – the network circle

By looking at our relationships it is possible to look at ourselves from the outside and see what resources we have in our network.

What to do?

Complete a network circle with the child. The exercise helps sharpen the child's attention and awareness of himself in relation to significant others.

Think about the people you know. Draw or write them in the circle, depending on how close you feel to them.

You can also ask the child where he wants the significant others to go in the circle – should they be closer, farther away, and who can help with that?

Example

A nine-year-old girl discovers that she feels closer to a neighbour that babysits her than she does to her mother.

She is both sad and happy that she has found an adult who is there for her.

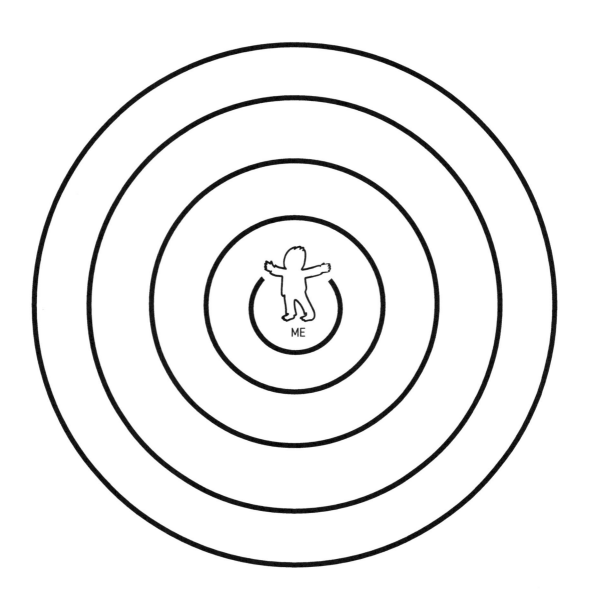

ME

Obtaining skills – relationships – a yin and yang balance

A fragile ability to mentalize is often closely associated with those who see the world as being black or white. The imbalance of only to see themselves as good and others as evil – or vice versa – is described in depth in the literature on borderline and mentalization. The following exercise is designed to help create more balance.

What to do?

Use the model with the child and say: "Sometimes it seems impossible to see anything else than the bad in another person and other times it seems impossible to see anything than the good."

Try to remember the good you feel when trapped inside the bad – and vice versa – as the yin and yang symbol: see the white in the black and black in the white.

Tips and tricks

With adults, ask them to think about the politician they dislike the most. With children, ask them about the last time they were really angry with someone.

Example

A fifteen-year-old boy is furious with his best friend, who has been with his girlfriend.

Using the model makes it possible to talk with him about how he still cares about his friend and actually misses him even though he is still mad at him.

MODEL A YIN AND YANG BALANCE

Think of a person you right now only think badly about. Who is it?

_____

Try to think of something good about that person.

_____

Now think of a person you only think good things about. Who is it?

_____

Try to think of something bad about that person.

_____

Resource focus – the shield of self-esteem

When working with neglected and traumatised children, it important to do concrete work at identifying their resources. In order to have a coherent positive sense of self, it is important that the child's strong sides are positively mirrored/reflected back to him. Vulnerable children have often had the experience of others only saying something positive in order to manipulate them. They can be very sceptical of praise.

This does not mean that they shouldn't encounter adults who reflect their positive aspects, but it makes special demands on professionals to be honest and sincere when discussing a child's specific resources, so that the child will have new experiences of being mirrored in a positive light.

What to do?

Tell the child that self-esteem is his shield against life's challenges. Ask the child to do the following: "Write or draw on each of the four parts of your personal shield of self-esteem."

1. What do I like about myself?
2. What I am good at?
3. What do others say I am good at?
4. What do I want for the future if I can have it any way I want?

Tips and tricks

Older children and adolescents might find the list of questions connected to the self-esteem shield a bit childish. But we are never too old to work on focusing our resources with another. It is important that the model be completed in writing – preferably with drawings – so that the child has a tangible visualisation of his resources.

> **Example**
> An eleven-year-old boy completes the self-esteem shield. It's hard for him to get started, but once finished, he says: "Imagine, I did not think there was anything nice to say about myself, but all of those things are correct."

MODEL THE SHIELD OF SELF-ESTEEM

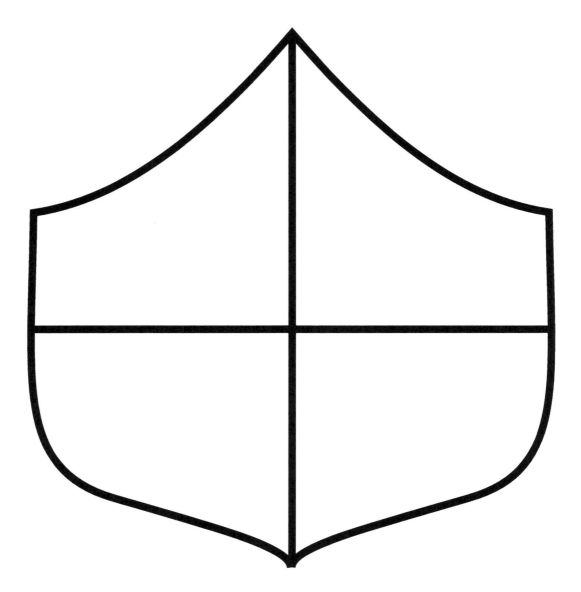

With inspiration from Blaustein & Kinniburgh, 2010

Resource focus – dreams for the future

The concept behind "dreams for the future" is to lift the child out of his current situation and into the future, giving him a sense of his own unrealised resources and potential. In these dreams for the future, things seem more possible and less out of reach than they may seem in the child's life at the moment. Through "dreams for the future" you can help the child create direction and hope in the reality the child is currently in the middle of/going through.

What to do?

The adult talks with the child about his dreams for the future. Ask the child where he sees himself when, for example, he is twenty-five years old. If he could plan his life exactly as he wanted it to be, what would his dream be? The exercise is about letting go and imagining the future exactly the way the child wants it – no matter how unrealistic it may seem. The adult asks for details and tries to make the dreams of the future as vivid as possible.

Tips and tricks

Remember to dream with the child and engage yourself in the process. Children and adolescents who have suffered neglect and trauma are often pessimistic when it comes to their future. Others often have very unrealistic ideas about their abilities, but these are welcome in this exercise where they are allowed to give their dreams all the energy they can.

Example

A sixteen-year-old girl who has just been convicted for violence does the exercise. She dreams of becoming a hairdresser and having her own flat and a small dog. At the time she does the exercise, the dream seems impossible. Six years later, the psychologist and the girl meet and she says that she never let go of her dream. Today it is a reality – despite the detours she faced, she achieved her dreams.

MODEL MY DREAMS FOR THE FUTURE

Where do you live?

_____

Are you married or have a significant other?

_____

What is your profession?

_____

Do you have children?

_____

Do you have pets?

_____

What is your relationship with your family?

_____

How have you conquered the challenges in your life to arrive at where you are today?

_____

Mentalization – doctor: what happens in the minds of others?

This model is often used in mentalization-based family therapy. It is used to increase curiosity in the different mental states inside the family.

What to do?

You will need a white coat and a stethoscope. The child alternates placing the stethoscope on the others present and guessing what they think/feel. The child is asked to go around to each family member and try to read their thoughts and feelings by putting the stethoscope to their brains. The therapist asks: "What is your mother thinking right now? See if the tool is working."

Tips and tricks

The exercise can also be done with a mobile phone, which is introduced as an "FBI tool" or an app that can read minds.

Example

An eleven-year-old boy comes along with his father to therapy. The father tells the psychologist that the boy has been given a "red card" for bad behaviour in school twice in the same day. When getting the red card twice, the student must sit in the principal's office for a whole day without speaking to anyone. The boy's father also had to come to the school and speak to the principal the following day.

The mood in the therapy room is unpleasant. The boy looks down at the table and the father stares out of the window. The psychologist takes out the stethoscope and white coat. The boy "reads" his father's thoughts. He says: "I can see you're disappointed in me and wish you had not worked so hard to get me home. You wish I had stayed with my grandmother in Iraq. You now think it makes sense that she beat me with a belt."

The father is very surprised and says that he thinks that he should have fought harder to get his boy home earlier and blames himself for his son getting the red cards.

Note: The exercise was developed by Eia Asen (Skårderud & Sommerfeldt, 2014) with inspiration from the Anna Freud Centre.

Mentalization – the hunt for mental states

This model is often used in mentalization-based family therapy. It is a good reminder that a person's behaviour is always a result of his underlying mental condition.

What to do?

Find a lot of magazines and give the children a magnifying glass. Start the hunt for different mental conditions. For example, the children could find pictures showing different emotions. It is easiest to spot the feelings of the models in the magazines by looking at them through the magnifying glass. The children should find pictures that illustrate as many underlying emotional states as possible.

Tips and tricks

The exercise can also be used to talk about the dimensions of mentalization. How can you see from the outside that she is happy inside (internal/external)? How can you sometimes just know how others feel? When is it necessary to make an effort in order to understand the other person (automatic/controlled)? How can two people feel differently (self/other)?

Example
A group of sexually abused girls is looking at the pictures, and they find an image with a girl lying with her face in the lap of a boy. The girls each react to the picture differently. One said, "She is being forced to give him oral sex." Another said, "He is comforting her." And the third said, "It's just two lovers, there is nothing wrong with having the desire to please each other, even if you have been sexually assaulted."

Note: The exercise was developed with inspiration from the Anna Freud Centre.

Mentalization – role play

This exercise is often used in mentalization-based family therapy. Role play can be used with families where interaction patterns between the individual members feel deadlocked and played out mechanically. Family members can experiment with those patterns by swapping roles and playing each other in order to increase understanding of how each one looks from the outside and what the other family member may have at stake, on the inside. Role playing can be very useful in families where the emotional temperature is too low, that is, a family that talks and talks about the same situation without commitment or an appropriate emotional response.

What to do?

If the emotional temperature allows room for it, ask the family members to switch roles and try to play each other. In this way, each one tries out the other's "mental shoes".

Tips and tricks

Be aware that role playing can feel awkward to some people and will require a little courage and practice. Be the role model for a playful, committed, and humorous approach. Children, however, often think it is fun to have an opportunity to play their parents.

Involve the physical space so that participants literally sit in each other's chairs. Remember to be in the mental shoes of others and include all family members by asking both participants and spectators how they felt about the role playing exercise. Spectators can also be given the task of awarding the participants points for how well they play the role of other family members. The purpose of the role play is to stimulate all-round mentalization.

Example

The divorced parents of two girls, aged fourteen and eleven, often end up in a discussion about visitation, because the girls' hobbies and desire to be with their friends often means that they have difficulty in visiting their father quite as often as the parents had agreed upon. The mother thinks the father gives up on his visitation rights too easily and does not take responsibility for maintaining close contact with the girls or sharing parental duties with her. The father feels that the mother does not respect the girls' desires to be free to do things that interest them, and that she is mostly just worried that it is extra work for her. After swapping roles, both parents say that they had to slow down in order to really empathise with the other's role. The father realises that the mother might be afraid that he is disappearing too quickly from the girls' lives, and the mother discovers that dad may be afraid that the girls might feel pressured to do things that are costly to them, just to make the parents happy.

Note: This exercise was developed in collaboration with a psychotherapist and BA in philosophy, Mette Mørk, and inspired by Anna Freud Centre.

Mentalization – the journalist game

This is a game that is often used in mentalization-based family therapy. The game is designed as an opportunity to investigate the mental states of other family members.

What to do?
The game is "television". The parents are "inside the television" and the children are journalists who can call in and ask about anything.

Tips and tricks
Make the exercise as playful as possible. The parents should sit close to one another, as if they were inside a TV set. The children may ask about anything that comes to mind, including their parents' own childhood: "How did mom feel when her father scolded her when she was young?"

Example
A family of five is in family therapy. The sixteen-year-old daughter is very self-destructive. It is agreed that the children can each play journalists and call in and ask the parents what it does to them when the daughter cuts herself. The sixteen year old takes part in the game, but does not want to be a journalist. She will be part of the audience watching the parents on TV instead.

The children take turns asking their parents about everything:

- How does the father feel when his daughter cuts herself?
- What is he thinking?
- What is he feeling?
- What about the mother? How does she feel when she yells at her daughter?
- What does the mother believe causes the daughter to cut herself?
- What feelings do the wounds on the daughter's arms awaken in the mother?

Note: The model was developed in collaboration with psychologist Anne Agerbo and inspired by Anna Freud Centre.

Mentalization – spin the bottle

In mentalization-based therapy, emotions are believed to be the "royal route to mentalizing". Therefore, it is a central part of family therapy to work with recognising your own feelings as well as the feelings of each member of the family.

What to do?

Write all the emotions that the child recognises on pieces of paper. Place the feelings in a circle with a soda bottle in the middle. The child spins the bottle, picks up the feeling it points to, and displays that emotion. The game can be expanded to show how other family members express the emotion.

Tips and tricks

Ask the family's youngest child what emotions he recognises and have him write them down on several pieces of paper.

> ### Example
> In a family that is very concerned about a daughter's eating disorder, the game quickly becomes centred on anxiety. At first the girl shows the emotion and the way she displays it, it is almost unrecognisable. The girl then tries to show how she experiences her mother when her mother is afraid. It is obvious that the mother is affected by this. The exercise gives rise to an important conversation about anxiety, worry, and eating.

Note: The exercise was developed in collaboration with psychologist Anne Agerbo and inspired by Anna Freud Centre.

Mentalization – my boundaries

Some children and adolescents have difficulty with the balance between themselves and others. They are too little aware of how they feel themselves and too consumed with how others feel. Or it becomes unclear who has which feelings, needs, and goals. It can be effective to do exercises about challenging the experience of the child's own boundaries and the right to feel own feelings and needs.

What to do?

You will need pieces of yarn of different colours. The child chooses a colour and makes a boundary around himself with the yarn. The child pays attention to how it feels to stand behind his limits. The therapist moves towards the yarn boundary and the child says "No" when the boundary is crossed. The exercise can reveal where in the body the child experiences his boundaries. The child "butterfly hugs" himself by crossing his arms and gently touching the opposite arm and saying, "I have a right to know where my limits are."

Tips and tricks

The exercise is particularly useful with children who have experienced sexual abuse. Sexual abuse is always a violation of the child's boundaries. These children have often lived in environments where their own needs and the needs of adults have been confused.

Example

An eight-year-old girl chooses red yarn to make a boundary around herself. The psychologist goes to the edge of the boundary and the girl says nothing as the psychologist crosses the yarn. This gives rise to new attempts and conversation about what the girl is feeling and what the psychologist experiences when the girl says "No" in a loud, clear voice.

MODEL **MY BOUNDARIES**

Draw borders on the figure as they apply to different people in your life. Here are some suggestions for types of borders:

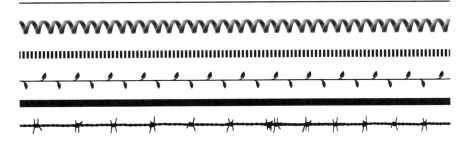

Mentalization – thought bubbles

"Thought bubbles" is a family therapy exercise designed to maintain attention on the mental states of the family.

What to do?

Thought bubbles can be used when the professional discovers that there is a need to cool down emotions in a situation that has escalated. Introduce the exercise when everyone in the group is less agitated.

Everyone is given a thought bubble. The professional chooses the first person to be "on".

That person is "the thinker". The others are "guessers".

The thinker writes his thoughts and feelings about the situation in his thought bubble.

The guessers write in their own thought bubbles what they believe the thinker was thinking and feeling. The guessers show their thought bubbles so that everyone in the group can see them.

Finally, the thinker shows his thought bubble, revealing what he actually felt and thought.

The guesses are then revealed to be correct, incorrect, off the mark, or close.

Tips and tricks

The model can be printed and laminated so it can be used again and again. Thoughts and feelings can be erased, so it also indirectly illustrates that thoughts and feelings can change.

Example

A family of different ethnic background than Danish is in family therapy. The father of the family is very angry with his daughter, whom he believes has adopted a lifestyle and clothing that are "too Danish". The family practitioner decides that the father will be the first thinker, since he already feels that his authority with his daughter has been undermined. The father is very surprised when his daughter and other family members guess his thoughts. This leads to him being curious about what will happen when it is his daughter's chance to be the thinker.

Note: The exercise was developed in collaboration with psychologist Anne Agerbo and inspired by Anna Freud Centre.

MODEL **THOUGHT BUBBLE**

Mentalization – the dream journey

The dream journey can be used to help a child gain a sense of internal security (Elklit, 2009).

What to do?

You can do visualisation exercises as an individual treatment or group therapy. There must be a sense of calm and security and the child should be lying on a mattress on the floor. The curtains can be closed. The child is led into his dream journey with a reading found on the next page.

Tips and tricks

Immediately following the exercise, the child can perhaps draw a picture of the place he travelled to during the dream journey. Later, the child can look at the drawing while in a safe place and give himself a "butterfly hug" by crossing his arms in front of his chest and touching himself on each shoulder. The child can be taught that he can find his way to a safe place when he needs to and can help his body remember that safe place by giving himself a butterfly hug.

Example

A twelve-year-old girl with a cleft palate has a fear of needles and is working in therapy to overcome that fear. Part of the treatment is to find a safe place that the girl can go the next time she needs to be given anaesthesia for an operation, and to find that safe place via a butterfly hug.

MODEL **MY DREAM JOURNEY**

Sit or lie as comfortably as possible. Relax as much as you can. Close your eyes. Breathe deeply through your nose, down into your abdomen and breathe out through your mouth. Do it again and feel your entire body relaxing. And one more time – and feel yourself relaxing …:

in your head

in your shoulders

in your arms

in your upper body

in your stomach

in your lower back

in your thighs

in your knees

in your feet

and all the way out into your toes.

Now think of a pleasant place to be, a nice place, a place where you feel safe and protected. It can be a place outside or inside – it can be a place you know – or somewhere in your imagination. It should be a comfortable place to be. Stay in this place. Try to notice what is happening around you. Notice the colours – perhaps there are many colours, maybe there is no colour. Notice the sounds – maybe you can hear animals or people, perhaps it is quiet. Notice the smells – maybe it smells pleasant, maybe there are no smells. Breathe deeply into your stomach and enjoy being in this place where you are safe and secure. Remember that this is your place, a place where you feel strong and safe. Remember, you can always return to this place in your mind, whether you are alone or with others – at home or away. Just close your eyes and think of your safe place.

With your eyes closed, imagine that you have found something special. Something that someone who loves you has left behind, just for you. You can pick it up and hold it in your hand. When you feel it in your hand, you think about the person who cares for you and left it for you.

You may now leave your safe place in your thoughts and slowly open your eyes. Let every part of your body awaken. Feel a relaxation and wellness in your entire body.

References

Ainsworth, M. & Bell, S.M. (1970). Attachment, exploration, and separation – illustrated by the behavior of one year olds in a strange situation. *Child Development*, 41(1): 49-67.

Akasha, S.E. & Olsen, A.-M. (2006). Sov godt. Copenhagen: Politikens Forlag.

Allen, J.G. (2013). Restoring mentalizing in Attachment relationships. Treating Trauma with plain old therapy. London: American Psychiatric Publishing.

Allen, J.G. (2014). Mentalisering i tilknytningsrelationer – *Behandling af traumer med traditionel terapi*. Copenhagen: Hans Reitzels Forlag.

Allen, J.G., Bleiberg, G. & Haslam-Hopwood, T. (2003). Mentalizing as a compass for treatment. *Bulletin of The Menninger Clinic*, Houston, Texas.

Allen, J.G. & Fonagy, P. (2006). *Handbook of Mentalization-Based Treatment*. Chichester, UK: Wiley & Sons.

Allen, J.G., Fonagy, P. & Bateman, A. (2010). *Mentalisering i klinisk praksis*. Copenhagen: Hans Reitzels Forlag.

American Psychiatric Association (1994). *Diagnostic and Statistical Manual of Mental Disorders IV*. Washington, DC: Author.

American Psychiatric Association (2014). *Diagnostiske kriterier DSM-5. Håndbog*. Virum, Denmark: Hogrefe Psykologisk Forlag.

Andersen, T.K. & Holter, H. (1997). Jeg vil jo ikke kalle mamma en fyllik. *Fokus*, 2: 124-134.

Bateman, A. & Fonagy, P. (2007). *Mentaliseringsbaseret behandling af borderline personlighedsforstyrrelse – En praktisk guide*. Copenhagen: Akademisk Forlag.

Bateman, A. & Fonagy, P. (2008). Eight-year follow-up of patients treated for borderline personality disorder – mentalization-based treatment versus treatment as usual. *American Journal of Psychiatry*, 165(5): 631-638.

Bateman, A. & Fonagy, P. (2012). *Handbook of Mentalization in Mental Health Practice*. Washington, DC: American Psychiatric Publishing.

Behrens, K.Y., Hesse, E. & Main, M. (2007). Mothers' attachment status as determined by the Adult Attachment Interview predicts their six year olds' reunion responses – a study conducted in Japan. *Developmental Psychology*, 43(6): 1553.

Berk, L. (1994). *Child Development.* Boston, MA: Allyn & Bacon.

Bevington, D. (2011). *AMBIT.* London: Anna Freud Centre.

Blaustein, E.M. (Ed.) (2006). *Children with Disrupted Attachment – A Video Series on Attachment Disorder.* Nevada City, CA: Cavalcade Productions.

Blaustein, M. & Kinniburgh, K. (2010). *Treating Traumatic Stress in Children and Adolescents.* New York: Guilford Press.

Bloom, S.L. (2005). The sanctuary model of organizational change for children's residential treatment therapeutic community. *International Journal for Therapeutic and Supportive Organizations, 26*(1): 65-81.

Bowlby, J. (1969). *Attachment – Attachment and Loss.* New York: Basic Books.

Bowlby, J. (1980). *Loss – Sadness and Depression – Attachment and Loss (volume 3).* London: Hogarth.

Cameron, R.J. & Maginn, C. (2010). *Achieving Positive Outcomes for Children in Care.* London: Lucky Duck.

Christoffersen, M.N. & DePanfilis, D. (2009). Prevention of child abuse and neglect and improvements. *Child Development Child Abuse Review, 18*: 24-40.

Cohen, J.A., Deblinger, E., Maedel, A.B. & Stauffer, L.B. (1999). Examining sex-related thoughts and feelings of sexually abused children and non-abused children. *Journal of Interpersonal Violence, 14*(7): 701-712.

Cohen, J.A., Mannarino, A.P. & Deblinger, E. (2006). *Treating Trauma and Traumatic Grief in Children and Adolescents.* New York: Guilford Press.

D'Andrea, W., Stolbach, B., Ford, J., Spinazzola, J. & van der Kolk, B. (2012). Understanding interpersonal trauma in children – why we need a developmentally appropriate trauma diagnosis. *American Journal of Orthopsychiatry, 82*(2): 187-200.

Dunn, J. & Brown, J. (2001). Emotion, pragmatics, and social understanding in the preschool years. In: D. Bakhurst & S. Shanker (Eds.), *Jerome Bruner – Language, Culture and Self.* Thousand Oaks, CA: Sage.

Egelund, M., Abrahams, R., Jensen, B.Å., Jørgensen, P., Riber, J., Ruby, P. & Warhuus, L. (1997). *En forskel der gør en forskel.* Copenhagen: Hans Reitzels Forlag.

Elklit, A. (2009). *Traumekursus for børnene på Bakkeskolen efter fyrværkerikatastrofen i Seest ved Kolding.* Kolding, Denmark: Syddansk Universitet.

Feldman, R. (2009). *The Liar in Your Life.* London: Virgin.

Fonagy, P. & Allison, E. (2012). What is mentalization? The concept and its foundations in developmental research. In: N. Midgley & I. Vrouva (Eds.), *Minding the Child.* New York: Routledge.

Fonagy, P. & Allison, E. (2014). The role of mentalizing and epistemic trust in the therapeutic relationship. *Psychotherapy, 51*(3): 372-380.

Fonagy, P., Gergely, G., Jurist, E. & Target, M. (2007). *Affektregulering, mentalisering og selvets udvikling.* Copenhagen: Akademisk Forlag.

Friedman, M.J., Keane, T.M. & Resick, P.A. (2007). *Handbook of PTSD Science and Practice*. New York: Guilford Press.

Gottman, J.M., Katz, L.F. & Hooven, C. (1996). Parental meta-emotion philosophy and the emotional life of families – theoretical models and preliminary data. *Journal of Family Psychology, 10*(3): 243-268.

Greene, R.W. (2009). *Fortabt i skolen*. Copenhagen: Pressto.

Hagelquist, J.Ø. (2006). Seksuelt overgrebne piger. *Psykolog Nyt, 60*.

Hagelquist, J.Ø. (2012). *Mentalisering i mødet med udsatte børn*. Copenhagen: Hans Reitzels Forlag.

Hagelquist, J.Ø. & Skov, M.K. (2014). *Mentalisering i pædagogik og terapi*. Copenhagen: Hans Reitzels Forlag.

Hawkes, L. (2011). With you and me in mind – mentalization and transactional analysis. *Transactional Analysis Journal, 41*(3): 230-240.

Herman, J.L. (1995). *I voldens kølvand – Psykiske traumer og deres heling*. Copenhagen: Hans Reitzels Forlag.

Jacobsen, J.C. (2014). *Lærernes grundfaglighed – mentalisering som arbejdsredskab*. Værløse, Denmark: Billesø & Baltzer.

Jørgensen, G. & Hagmund-Hansen, C. (2013). *Børn i gode hænder*. Copenhagen: Hans Reitzels Forlag.

Karpman, S.B. (1968). Fairy tales and drama analysis. *Transactional Analysis Bulletin, 7*(26): 39-43.

Karpman, S.B. (2007). The New Drama Triangles. Presentation at the International Transactional Analysis Conference, San Francisco.

Karterud, S. & Bateman, A. (2011). *Mentaliseringsbaseret terapi – Manual og vurderingsskala*. Copenhagen: Hans Reitzels Forlag.

Kilpatrick, K.L. & Williams, L.M. (1997). Post-traumatic stress disorder in child witnesses to domestic violence. *American Journal of Orthopsychiatry, 67*(4): 639-644.

Kolk, B. van der (2005a). Developmental trauma disorder – towards a rational diagnosis for children with complex trauma histories. *Psychiatric Annals, 35*(5): 401-408.

Kolk, B. van der (2005b). Editorial introduction to child abuse and victimization. *Psychiatric Annals, 35*(5): 374-378.

Kolk, B. van der (2007). The Traumatized Child. Red Cross conference, 8 February.

Kolk, B. van der, Pynoos, R.S., Cicchetti, D., Cloitre, M., D'Andrea, W., Ford, J.D., Lieberman, A.F., Putnam, F.W., Saxe, G., Spinazzola, J., Stolbach, B.C. & Teicher, M. (2009). Proposal to Include a Developmental Trauma Disorder Diagnosis for Children and Adolescents in DSM-V. Available from: traumacenter. org/announcements DTD_NCTSN_official_submission_to_DSM_V_Final_ Version.pdf.

Larson, N. & Maddock, J. (1995). *Incestuous Families – An Ecological Approach to Understanding and Treatment.* New York: W. W. Norton.

Levine, P.A. (1998). *Væk tigeren – Helbredelse af traumer.* Copenhagen: Borgen.

Levine, P.A. & Kline, M. (2007). *Trauma through a Childs Eyes.* Berkeley, CA: North Atlantic.

MacLean, P.D. (1990). *The Triune Brain in Evolution – Role in Paleocerebral Functions.* New York: Plenum Press.

Main, M. & Hesse, E. (1990). Parents' unresolved traumatic experiences are related to infant disorganized attachment status – is frightened/frightening parental behavior the linking mechanism? In: M. T. Greenberg, D. Cicchetti, & E. M. Cummings (Eds.), *Attachment in the Preschool Years – Theory, Research, and Intervention.* Chicago, IL: University of Chicago Press.

Midgley, N. & Vrouva, I. (Eds.) (2012). *Minding the Child – Mentalization-Based Interventions with Children, Young People and their Families.* London: Routledge.

Perry, B.D. & Szalavitz, M. (2011). *Drengen der voksede op som hund.* Copenhagen: Hans Reitzels Forlag.

Peterson, K.C., Prout, M.F. & Schwartz, R.A. (1991). *Post-Traumatic Stress Disorder – A Clinical Guide.* New York: Plenum Press.

Pughe, B. & Philpot, T. (2007). *Living alongside a Child's Recovery, Therapeutic Parenting with Traumatized Children.* London: Jessica Kingsley.

Rossouw, T. (2012). *Mentalization-Based Treatment for Adolescence (MBT-A).* Course. London: Anna Freud Centre.

Ryden, G. & Wallroth, P. (2010). *Mentalisering – at lege med virkeligheden.* Copenhagen: Hans Reitzels Forlag.

Schiraldi, G.R. (2000). *The Posttraumatic Stress Disorder.* New York: McGraw-Hill.

Siegel, D.J. & Bryson, T.P. (2014). *No-drama discipline.* New York: Bantam.

Siegel, D.J. & Hartzell, M. (2006). *Forældre indefra.* Copenhagen: Akademisk Forlag.

Skårderud, F. & Sommerfeldt, B. (2014). *Miljøterapibogen – Mentalisering som holdning og handling.* Copenhagen: Hans Reitzels Forlag.

Sørensen, J.H. (2009). *Mentaliseringsbaseret behandling i teori og praksis.* Copenhagen: Hans Reitzels Forlag.

Stern, D.N., Bruschweiler-Stern, N. & Freeland, A. (1999). *En mor bliver til.* Copenhagen: Hans Reitzels Forlag.

Webster-Stratton, C. (2009). *De utrolige år.* Frederiksberg, Denmark: Frydenlund.

About the author

 **Janne Østergaard Hagelquist** is a licensed psychologist and certified as a specialist in child psychology and supervision. Most of her work has dealt with the treatment, supervision, and education of neglected and traumatised children, adolescents, and adults.

In recent years, she has been particularly concerned with improving knowledge about the meaning of trauma and the effects of using mentalization in the treatment, education, and working relationships dealing with trauma. She works to disseminate psychological knowledge in a way that is easily understandable and useful. Janne Østergaard Hagelquist founded the Center for Mentalization, which aims to spread knowledge about mentalizing and the use of mentalization-based therapy (see more at www.centerformentalisering.dk or the Facebook page for the Center for Mentalization).

In 2012 she published the book *Mentalisering i mødet med udsatte børn.* In 2014, in cooperation with Marianne Køhler Skov, she released *Mentalisering i pædagogik og terapi.* A further work, *Mentalisering i organisationer* was published in 2016 in cooperation with Heino Rasmussen.